Christ For The Nations
The Golden Jubilee

The pages of this book contain the account of God's faithfulness and the glorious works He has accomplished through men and women dedicated to taking the Gospel of Jesus Christ to the four corners of the earth.

The ministry began with the inspiration to print *The Voice of Healing* magazine some 50 years ago to broadcast the healing evangelistic crusades through which God was moving so mightily. As that wave of the Spirit began to subside, Gordon Lindsay turned his eyes toward the nations of the world, and in 1967, the name was changed to Christ For The Nations to signify its global vision.

CFN is known for its many-faceted ministry—through its Native Church Foundation, literature, relief, support of orphanages, and much more. With the founding of Christ For The Nations Institute in 1970, came the means of training men and women to evangelize and disciple the peoples of the world. Today, most of the 26,000 alumni can be found working for the Lord, both in the ministry and in the marketplace.

Excerpts...

"They heard. They saw. It began to happen. ... Subscriptions doubled. Instead of wanting their dollar back, subscribers were sending two ... ."

"One day in the spring of 1970, having been in prayer, Gordon said to Freda, "We should start a Bible school." Freda and all three of the children were reluctant, but Gordon's vision won out. That very fall, the interdenominational Bible training center was inaugurated."

"We anticipate that the dynamic foundation of integrity and vision that has been laid in the last 50 years will result in a spiritually synergistic force that will impact every nation for Christ in the 21st century."

Christ For The Nations

50 Years

1 9 4 8 - 1 9 9 8

In 1998, Christ For The Nations in Dallas, Texas, and the state of Israel are both celebrating...

The Year of Jubilee

Christ For The Nations — The Golden Jubilee
ISBN 0-89985-500-8

Published by Christ For The Nations, Inc.
P.O. Box 769000, Dallas, TX 75376-9000

Foreword

50 Years of Identifying With the King's Heart

Christ For The Nations is now a half a century young. From the first *Voice of Healing* publication to its present worldwide ministry that touches millions of lives, the message has always been the same: "Go ye!" That message came from the heart of God, and He instilled that mission in the hearts of my parents, Gordon and Freda Lindsay.

The vision was born in the spirit of revival that was sweeping North America following World War II. As a result of Dad and Mom's obedient and steadfast response, multitudes have been blessed. When Dad graduated to heaven 25 years ago, Mom took up the torch and carried it relentlessly for another 25 years. Her faithfulness to the vision has been an inspiration to many, including my wife, Ginger and me.

I believe CFN has prevailed for the last 50 years because its purpose was birthed in the heart of God. Our passion at CFN is to be obedient to the Great Commission — to harvest sons and daughters into the family of God, disciple them in His ways, and then train them to reproduce themselves.

The ministry was not built on gifted nor charismatic personalities, but simply managed by faithful stewards with the character, heart and vision of the Father. Because of this solid foundation, those who have served the body of Christ at CFN have been more restrained than most in the areas of pride, competition and selfish ambition. And these servant leaders have been awarded God's giftings, anointing and provision to convey His love to the peoples of the world.

As we serve anticipating Christ's return, may we never resort to using human wisdom to instigate "revival." May we never have to discover that doing God's work that way may be deadly — as King David did when he undertook taking back to Israel the Ark of the Covenant on a new cart rather than on the shoulders of the priests as God had instructed. Instead, may we seek to know the Father's heart so that the anointing will remain strong upon every facet of the ministry and upon every man and woman of God serving Him therein.

This volume is a record of God working through servant leaders for 50 years. Those of us who are presently serving at CFN have purposed in our hearts to continue to facilitate the message on God's heart. We are eager to carry the torch into the new millennium. We are determined to run the race, not for the glory of man, but for the pleasure of the Father and the glory of His Son, Jesus Christ!

Dennis Lindsay,
Chairman of the Board, President & CEO

Christ For The Nations, Inc.
Board of Directors

Edward Bianchi

Guy Branham

Dr. James Garlow

John Heffner

Freda Lindsay

Dennis Lindsay

Gilbert Lindsay

Sam Monzingo

Taylor Nichols

John Packer

John Sluder

Don Spear

Doug Taylor

E.C. McKenzie

Wylie Vale

Acknowledgements

To FREDA LINDSAY — CFN co-founder, chairman of the board emeritus, and editor — for writing the Introduction and assisting with the writing and editing "The Fruit" section.

To DENNIS LINDSAY — CFN Chairman of the Board, President and CEO — for writing the Foreword and "The Vision" section.

To ANNA JEANNE PRICE — our first managing editor and a key member of the music department for many years — for creatively sharing her wonderful memories, particularly in "The First 25 Years," "The Institute" (The Sounds of Worship, Music and the Arts), and "The Fruit" sections.

To R.J. KOLAND — CFN development director — for his contributions, particularly in "The Vision" section.

To PATTI CONN — CFN managing editor and yearbook advisor — for her writing, editing, organizing and general oversight of this entire project.

Managing Editor's Note:

I would like to personally thank several staff members who have helped with this project. First of all, CFN's Editorial Department Staff: Chris Renwick (assistant to the managing editor), Julie Holmquist (editorial assistant), Melissa Walken (office assistant) and Mayra Salazar (graphic designer). For this special project, several other CFN staff members have assisted: Nickie and Sandi Geldenhuys, Naomi Westbrook, Arlene Friesen, Christopher Holt and Dr. Duane Weis.

I would also like to thank Swyers Printing for their assistance with the typesetting and design.

It is with happy hearts that we present this pictorial history of Christ For The Nations. The pleasant task of reaching back into volumes of early magazines, flipping through yearbooks, pulling out photo files that draw tears and smiles, have brought a renewed sense of awe and appreciation for the guiding hand of God, and for the people through which He worked; imperfect, yet chosen. A new "high" – inspiration and faith for the future – is the sweet reward for the many hours of labor.

At the same time, our elation has a downside. For every person named, there could be ten others as deserving. How we wished to include more! But such limitations as time, space, available information, conservative budget, and other factors, held us in check whenever our dreamy production plans edged toward unreality. Besides, to do justice to 50 phenomenal years, the book would be too heavy to carry home!

A famous writer made comments to which we can relate, as he faced a similar dilemma two millennia ago. He created unforgettable word-pictures, poignantly describing several generations of heroes of faith, from Abel to Rahab. Then he apologized for not having time to pay individual tribute to a host of others. We refer, of course to the writer of Hebrews 11.

However, God keeps perfect records. He knows the name and the sacrifice of the many dedicated faculty and staff, the generosity of many saints whose contributions made all this possible, and of the tens of thousands of alumni who are impacting their worlds of influence. To all of these, we say thank you for being a part of our lives and for letting us be a part of yours.

—The Editors

Table of Contents

Introduction . . . . *viii*

The Lindsays 1

The First 25 Years 23

The Second 25 Years 45

The Institute 71

The External Ministries 105

The Fruit 117

The Vision 143

Introduction

The sons of Issachar ... had understanding of the times, to know what Israel ought to do (I Chr. 12:32).

Gordon Lindsay

As the Christian world watched, one by one the "giants" of the miracle healing ministry passed from the scene: Smith Wigglesworth, Dr. Charles Price, Maria Woodworth-Etter, Aimee Semple McPherson, and others. Since God knows and watches the times and seasons, whom would the Lord use to carry on with these supernatural giftings?

The Lord has always had leaders in training so the torch of faith can be passed from one generation to another. Joshua followed Moses. Elisha succeeded Elijah. And an unknown evangelist and young writer, my husband, Gordon Lindsay, from Portland, Oregon, would be uniquely used to fan the flames of revival and faith following World War II.

Coming out of obscurity, Gordon supported and promoted the ministries of many others, then the Lord began using him significantly. Through his revival services, writings, and ministers' conventions, he started encouraging pastors and evangelists everywhere to walk in bold faith. The tent meetings, open-air services, and revivals in auditoriums that multiplied across America were characterized by dramatic conversions and healings. Gordon's anointed writing skills recorded what God was so powerfully doing in a magazine called, *The Voice of Healing*. The initial copy was printed April 1, 1948, and it has continued uninterrupted each month for the past 50 years. Since 1967, both the ministry and the magazine have been known as Christ For The Nations.

Gordon was born during a mighty revival in Zion City, Illinois, on June 18, 1906. His parents attended the Dr. John Alexander Dowie and Dr. John G. Lake revivals and instilled in him a powerful faith in God for the supernatural.

Gordon was an avid student, reading thousands of books. He knew the Bible from cover to cover. He became "a walking encyclopedia," and could converse intelligently on many subjects.

He had a keen love for and interest in Israel. When someone would accuse him, "You're just pro-Israel," he would answer, "I'm just pro-Bible. Read the Bible."

Prayer was the "business" of Gordon's life. He would say, "Every day, I drive the devil back a little further." And, "When You own a business, you get up and go every day to attend to it, not just when you feel like it. So it is with prayer."

Integrity was Gordon's hallmark. He sought no glory for himself. He was quick to give others credit for what was being accomplished. He wisely said, "Few ministers can properly handle popularity, power or prosperity." Gordon was willing to sell our home and place the money into the new CFN Bible school. He lived the sacrificial message he proclaimed. His personal bank account had little more than enough to pay for his funeral. His treasures were laid up in heaven.

Gordon laid strong foundations upon which others, also called of God, could and would continue to build. Myself, our three children, their spouses, and eight grandchildren are all serving the Lord today. The dedicated staff of Christ For The Nations, past and present, have also built upon these foundations. With God's help, we are together reaching the nations with the Gospel.

This book helps to tell the incredible story of faith and the unbelievable faithfulness of God over these past 50 years.

Freda Lindsay

Freda Lindsay,
Co-founder, Christ For The Nations

The Lindsays

GORDON AND FREDA LINDSAY helped inaugurate the ministry now known as Christ For The Nations. Their vision and perseverance has impacted 120 nations of the world. When Gordon went to heaven 25 years ago, Freda picked up the torch, and with great determination, ran with it. She is living proof that God uses women to build His Kingdom.

Today the Lindsays' youngest son, Dennis, who has been a faculty member since 1973, is CFN's chairman of the board, president and CEO. The Lindsays' first child, Shira, has been serving the Lord in Israel for more than 30 years. Their oldest son, Gilbert, a printer, is today printing millions of Bibles and other Christian literature on once-communist presses in Belarus.

Gordon & Freda,
the newlyweds

Lindsay family

Dennis

Carole

Gilbert

Gordon's Early Years

Gordon's parents, Thomas and Effie

TO THE YOUNG GORDON LINDSAY (1906-1973), the traditional church in his hometown of Portland, Oregon, seemed dull compared to science, astronomy and fascinating new inventions such as radio. The church's influence was weak, and his carnal inclinations were strong. Where were the miracles he read about in the Bible, and why were ministers namby-pamby rather than full of faith and action?

At the age of 19, Gordon reluctantly attended a revival at Dr. Lake's Portland church to please his mother, whom he loved and respected. The atmosphere was electric – a striking contrast to the dull services to which he was accustomed. Hanging on the walls of the building was a curious collection of crutches, braces, casts, etc. that had been discarded by people who had been miraculously healed. Gordon decided this was either base deception or something worth looking into.

The speaker, Charles Parham, not only possessed a powerful anointing, but keenness of mind, eloquence and wit. Night after night, Parham's powerful preaching dealt devastating blows to Gordon's worldly philosophy of life, but his carnal nature

Gordon at 3, with his sister, Gladys

defied surrender of his will to God's until finally one night he could no longer resist. Realizing his sinful life had offended God, a fountain of tears gushed forth as he repented at the altar. When he stood to his feet, he had not only an assurance that God had saved him and a realization that he was beginning a new life, but a call to preach the Gospel.

Gordon began to pray for a ministry that would reach the multitudes. He eagerly read every book he could find on apostolic ministry. Realizing the importance of prayer, and the helplessness of man to combat the powers of darkness on his own, he sometimes waited on the Lord all night, asking for a visitation of His mighty power.

During the year following Gordon's conversion, two remarkable evangelistic campaigns were held in the Portland Church. The first was held by Billy Sunday, an orator with a down-to-earth way of dealing with common man. Using pungent and expressive language delivered in a rapid-fire manner, he influenced thousands to accept Christ.

Shortly after this campaign, noted evangelist Dr. Charles S. Price was brought to town. But because of strong opposition from denominational circles, Dr. Price was forced to terminate his campaign after only a couple of weeks of meetings.

In the Portland Church, prophecies began to come forth that there would soon be a great move of the Spirit with signs, wonders and miracles. With a fire burning in his heart to minister, Gordon, along with two other young men, started on the evangelistic field. They set up a tent and held meetings in El Cajon, California. By the end of their meetings there, they had won a number of souls, learned a few hard lessons, and come to the realization that they were very inexperienced.

As the campaign was drawing to a close, Gordon was stricken with an almost fatal case of ptomaine poisoning. Hearing of Gordon's condition, Dr. Lake had him brought the 16 miles to his home in San Diego. Continuing to weaken in body and wracked with constant pain, Gordon had recurring thoughts that death was approaching. He began to read some typed sermons on healing by Dr. Lake, which Mrs. Lake had given him. He began to understand the difference between passive and active faith. When the light dawned on him that he must act on the Word of God, he got up from his bed. As his feet touched the

Gordon (extreme left) with his high school graduating class

floor, he began to praise the Lord for his healing. At that instant his cramps vanished, and for the first time in many days, he felt hungry. He had learned not only that faith must be acted upon, but that God's best for His children is divine health (Ex. 15:26) rather than divine healing.

Returning to Portland, Gordon gave himself to prayer, study of the Word, and reading books about great soul winners of the past. Soon he found himself again on the evangelistic field. During his twenties, Gordon held many evangelistic campaigns in different cities. Sometimes there were many conversions, sometimes only a few. In 1932 while visiting his home, he held several nights of meetings in the diminishing Portland Church, which was now without a pastor since Dr. Lake had moved to San Diego to start a mission there. Only one young woman was converted on the final night – Freda Schimpf, who five years later became his wife.

The Thomas Lindsay family photo taken shortly after Gordon's (upper left) high school graduation

Freda's Early Years

Freda at age 6 with her two younger sisters, Edith and Elma

THE NIGHT FREDA SCHIMPF surrendered her life to the Lord, He spoke to her in a still, small voice and told her that if she would be faithful to Him, she would one day marry Gordon. She told no one, and during the next four years, saw Gordon only about once a year when he returned home to visit his family.

Freda, one of 12 children, was born on April 18, 1914 in a sod house on a large wheat farm her parents had homesteaded on the arid plains near Burstall, Saskatchewan, Canada. Her father was of German origin, and had grown up in German communities in Russia. By the time the next child was born, Freda's father, Gottfred, had built a large, beautiful, 10-room house. During World War I, the wheat market was favorable, and the ranch prospered. But Freda's mother, Kaity, did not like the harsh winters, since the temperature would dip to 60 degrees below zero. So she prevailed upon Gottfred to move to a warmer climate. Thus the family moved to Oregon City, Oregon in 1919 after selling the ranch and auctioning off all their household items and the cattle. The apple orchard her father purchased in Oregon turned out to be a financial disaster because of the post-war slump in the economy. In despair, Gottfred turned to God.

In Canada, Freda's family had attended a

Lutheran church, but in Oregon City, they were exposed to the Full Gospel for the first time. Freda's father and her older brothers

Freda's parents, Gottfred and Kaity Schimpf, with her brother Fred and sisters Esther and Emma.

and sisters were filled with the Spirit. But this blessed experience eluded her mother for 35 years, for she never felt she was good enough to attain such spiritual heights. Finally, when she heard an evangelist explain that the baptism in the Holy Spirit is a gift from God, she was filled that very day. Perhaps that is why Freda so enjoys encouraging believers to receive the gift of the Holy Spirit.

A year after moving to Oregon City, the family had to leave the farm. As Freda grew up, her life was filled with hardships. It took more than her father earned at his job at a lumber mill to feed a family of 14. Every summer, the family picked berries of every kind, plus beans, hops, etc. There was little time for play. At 13, Freda began to look for employment. That was the only way her father would permit her to attend high school. Being from the old school, he didn't believe women needed education past

Freda, shortly before her marriage

grammar school. Her first job was for a family nearby, for whom she cleaned, washed, ironed and cooked for a year. For the next several years, she worked for a Jewish family, where she received room, board, clothing and $15 a month. During those years she worked away from home, Freda strayed from her walk with God.

When Freda graduated from high school, she received a partial scholarship to the school of her choice. But there was no way she could afford to pay the remainder, so as fall 1932 came, she watched some of her friends go off to college, while she worked as a domestic.

One October afternoon, Freda's older sister, Molly, encouraged her to attend a revival meeting being held by a young evangelist, Gordon Lindsay. That night, Freda was gloriously converted.

After her conversion, Freda became actively involved in ministry as Crusader president of the 200 young people in the Portland Foursquare Gospel Church — helping lead the youth in prison ministry, street witnessing and directing the young people's meetings. Feeling she should prepare herself for the role of minister's wife so she could assist Gordon, Freda enrolled in the Foursquare Bible school's night classes, while she worked by day as a cashier in a large department store.

The Lindsays' Marriage, Family and Early Ministry

FOUR YEARS AFTER FREDA'S conversion, Gordon looked her up at work and asked her to dinner. Before he left a few days later, he asked if she would answer his letters if he wrote, and she, of course, agreed. Their relationship blossomed into love, and on Sunday night, November 14, 1937, they were married before 1,600 people by Dr. Harold Jeffries, pastor of the Portland Foursquare Church and that denomination's Northwest District superintendent.

After their wedding, the young couple traveled and returned to San Fernando, California where Gordon had started a church. Because Freda had only six months of schooling left before she

Gordon and Freda's wedding in 1937

would graduate, she and Gordon agreed that it would be advisable for her to complete her course. So that next January, he resigned his pastorate and returned to the evangelistic field while Freda finished her schooling at Life Bible College in Los Angeles.

After Freda graduated, the Lindsays were asked by Dr. Jeffries to help a church in Tacoma, Washington on an interim basis. A few months later, when a permanent pastor was located, they were asked to pioneer a church in Billings, Montana.

The church building in Billings wasn't finished, so Gordon and Freda worked feverishly to complete it. They felt the only way to reach the community was to go door to door, visiting with the people, ministering to their needs, and then inviting them to the evening services. Gordon played the piano and preached every night. For the first

Gordon (standing, second from right) with his family just before his marriage

Freda attending LIFE in Los Angeles in 1939

couple of months, Freda was the janitor, the Sunday school superintendent, the young people's leader, and the song director.

There was no heat in the tabernacle in Billings. After the winter snow melted, the spring rains set in and seeped into the church, and they found it impossible to dry out the sawdust floor. Their living quarters consisted of two rooms upstairs, and the roof was so slanted that they could only stand completely upright in the center of one room. The rooms were insufferably hot in the summer and cold in the winter.

Freda developed a bad cold. As the weeks went by, instead of getting better, her coughing increased and her weight dropped to 94 pounds. Gordon decided Freda needed rest, so they traveled the thousand miles to Portland so she could stay with her family, and Gordon returned to Billings. Resting at her mother's house did not help; instead, Freda's condition worsened by the day. One morning, Freda's sister came to her, weeping, and said, "Freda, we think you have tuberculosis." The dreaded word "tuberculosis" pierced Freda's heart, for the possibility had been haunting her. After she was X-rayed, the doctor gave her the bad news: She had tuberculosis in both lungs! He told her she must spend a year in bed, and that if her family could not give her

The newlyweds in front of their first church in San Fernando, California

constant care, he would arrange for her to enter a sanitarium.

Upon being notified of Freda's condition, Gordon again returned immediately the thousand miles (at 30 mph) to Portland. He encouraged Freda that it was God's will to heal her, quoting verse after verse of Scripture. He left her room with this final one: "Beloved, if our heart does not condemn us, we have confidence toward God" (I Jn. 3:21). After spending several hours with the Lord, asking His forgiveness and making certain there was nothing between her soul and her Savior, Freda knew she was ready to be healed.

That night, Gordon and Freda prayed the prayer of faith after which she arose from bed, declaring her healing. She did not "feel" healed at first, but continued to believe God. Two weeks later, they returned to Billings. For a few months, she occasionally had "symptoms," but Gordon had instructed her to resist with all her strength Satan's suggestions, which she did. And it worked. On April 18, 1998, Freda turned 84, and she's still going strong.

Gordon with the Lindsays' first child, Carole

The Lindsays spent the next several years on the evangelistic field.

The Lindsays at the church they pastored in Ashland, Oregon

In 1940, their first child, Carole Ann, was born. That same year, Gordon, who over the next 33 years became a prolific writer, produced his first of 250 books, *The Wonders of Bible Chronology*. Dr. John G. Lake had prophesied 15 years earlier that Gordon would one day write books that would be used as textbooks the world over. Gordon's books have been translated into 76 languages of which 13 of them are distributed to hundreds of thousands of eager recipients in developing nations through the Literature Crusade program.

In 1943, the Lindsays' second child, Gilbert, came along. A year later, with World War II having started and the resulting travel restrictions and financial concerns, the Lindsays decided to accept a call to pastor a small Assembly of God congregation in Ashland, Oregon. Having resolved to build up the church, the congregation doubled, tripled, then

Gordon and Freda with their children, Carole, Dennis and Gilbert.

quadrupled under their ministry. Their little family expanded, too; Dennis Gordon was born in 1946.

The Lindsays enjoyed pastoring in Ashland. In fact, one night shortly after Dennis' birth, Freda lay in bed one night, expressing her gratitude to the Lord for her beautiful family, the spacious parsonage, and a congregation that loved them dearly. She told the Lord she would be perfectly satisfied to remain there, so when the Rapture took place, He could look for the Lindsay family in Ashland!

But in 1948, Jack Moore, pastor and builder from Shreveport, Louisiana, who was a long-time friend of Gordon's, invited Gordon and Freda to go with him to attend a meeting of a Baptist minister by the name of William Branham. That trip completely changed the course of their lives. Gordon felt impressed to work with Branham and took a leave of absence from the church. Freda remained in Ashland to oversee it.

The Lindsay family all dressed up to attend a wedding

Messiah's Messengers

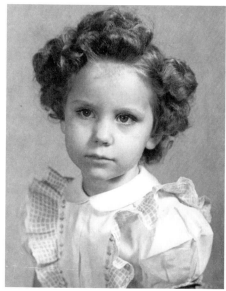

Carole (Shira) Lindsay

SHIRA *(CAROLE)*, THE OLDEST OF GORDON AND Freda's three children, met Ari Sorko-Ram in Hollywood while she was recruiting American Jews to emigrate to Israel.

Shira earned her bachelor's at Southern Methodist University in Dallas, modeled in Texas and Spain, made several documentary films, and is an accomplished pianist. Ari had attended the University of Southern California, played rugby for four years in France, professional football for St. Louis Cardinals, acted in 150 movies in Israel and Hollywood, and later became a County Sheriff.

Ari and Shira together have ministered in Israel since 1976 (Shira having served there since 1967). They are Israeli citizens, have two children, Ayal and Shani (20 and 19) who were born in Israel, and are presently in Bible training in Pensacola, Florida.

As Messianic Jews, Ari and Shira direct their own ministry, Maoz. They have pioneered Messianic Jewish congregations in the Tel Aviv area, have emphasized evangelism and the Spirit-filled life, and have overseen the translation and publication of several Gospel books in Hebrew. Shira has written for many publications concerning the Messianic Jewish Movement and the role with which Christians have been entrusted in Israel's spiritual resurrection. Their monthly newsletter giving the prophetic, political and spiritual perspective of current events in Israel is read by Christian leaders throughout the world for inside information about Israel which cannot be found in the secular media.

In the last few years, the Sorko-Rams have held three national pastors'

Shira meeting former prime minister, David Ben-Gurion — father of modern Israel

conferences, two with Jack Hayford, with about 80% of all Israel's local leaders and pastors attending. They have also held a national youth conference co-sponsored by six other Israeli congregational leaders and directed street evangelism campaigns, using drama and music, in cooperation with other pastors in Tel Aviv and Haifa.

Ari and Shira began a new congregation 2-1/2 years ago — strongly evangelistic in orientation. The last two years they have trained a core group of Israelis on a one-to-one basis, who are now being primed to work as cell leaders.

God has spoken specifically to their hearts to do three things to position themselves for the coming revival in Israel: 1) train Israeli leadership, 2) translate and publish basic discipleship materials and produce Hebrew language materials in video and audio, and 3) acquire a larger building from which they can evangelize, serve, nourish the new disciples, and administrate cell congregations.

This last year, in cooperation with King of Kings College, they began a leadership Bible school program for 20 Israelis from their congregation.

Ministry headquarters for the Maoz ministry is in Ramat HaSharon, Israel, a suburb of Tel Aviv. Their administrative office is located in Dallas, Texas, with additional offices in Canada, England and Germany. They are endorsed as a Messianic Jewish Ministry in Israel by the Union of Messianic Jewish Congregations, the Messianic Jewish Alliance, and churches and organizations around the world.

Shira and Ari Sorko-Ram married in 1977

Ari and Shira with son, Ayal, and daughter, Shani

Shira ministering in music on the streets of Tel Aviv

The Sorko-Rams

A Printing Pulpit

Gilbert Lindsay

Gilbert and Shirley married in 1971

GILBERT, THE MIDDLE OF THREE children born to Gordon and Freda Lindsay, attended Evangel College in Springfield, Missouri, and later graduated from Baylor University in Waco, Texas with a bachelor's in business.

On May 28, 1971, Gilbert Lindsay married Shirley Cowart. Daughter of Rev. and Mrs. L.W. Cowart, Shirley graduated from Southwestern Assemblies of God Bible College in Waxahatchie, Texas, and later from Texas Wesleyan University in Fort Worth, with a bachelor's in elementary education. She taught three years in Duncanville public schools. Gilbert and Shirley have three children: Michael, 25, Julia, 23, and Marcy, 20.

Gilbert has worked in the printing industry his entire career, starting out at an early age doing hand labor in his father's small printing shop. He owned and operated a printing plant in Dallas until he moved his entire production department to Minsk, Belarus to fulfill a need for printing the Good News in a part of the world that was "off limits" until just recently. He now heads one of the most unique printing facilities on the planet, in a building that was once the printing plant for the Academy of Science for the Soviet Republic of White Russia (Belarussia).

World Wide Printing and Publishing is the

Gilbert and Shirley with their three children Michael, Julia and Marcy

Gilbert at his printing plant in Minsk, Belarus

only Western-quality printing plant in the former Soviet Union. The plant has been operating since 1990, printing literature for 120 different Christian organizations. To date, over three million Bibles, 15 million New Testaments, and 80 million other pieces of Christian literature have been printed.

A sales office for World Wide Printing and Publishing is located in Duncanville, Texas. Michael is vice president of distribution and Julia is financial analyst. Marcy is a sophomore at Baylor University, majoring in marketing. Gilbert and Shirley travel extensively, making sales calls. Gilbert has been to Minsk 60 times. Shirley accompanies him twice a year.

The entire family are members of Calvary Temple in Dallas, Texas, whose pastor is Rev. Don George.

"Send us around the world with the news of your saving power and your eternal plan for all mankind." (Ps. 67:2 LB)

"And the gospel must first be published among all nations." (Mk. 13:10 KJV)

The Gilbert Lindsays

Carrying the Vision

Dennis Lindsay

Dennis and Ginger married in 1970

DENNIS GORDON, THE YOUNGEST OF Gordon and Freda Lindsay's three children, was born in Ashland, Oregon, where his parents were pastoring. The Lindsays' involvement in the healing crusades of the '50s took the family across the U.S. many times, providing Dennis a rich spiritual heritage as he witnessed the miraculous in his father's meetings.

Dennis graduated from Southern California College in Costa Mesa, where he majored in science. During his third year, participating in a life-changing YWAM summer outreach to the Caribbean caused him to add Bible as an additional major.

During the opening week festivities his senior year, at the college's "Dating Game," Ginger Krickbaum, a freshman psychology major, chose Dennis out of three eligible bachelors, and they quickly became sweethearts. Ginger worked for a season as Cinderella at Disneyland.

Upon graduation, Dennis joined Youth With A Mission in Switzerland, where he attended their School of Evangelism and ministered mostly in Spain. After a year, he travelled to California, where he and Ginger were married. Back in YWAM-Switzerland, Dennis became the work supervisor and Ginger completed the School of Evangelism course while working as a secretary to Loren Cunningham, YWAM's founder.

After completing YWAM's modular program, they spent an adventurous three years ministering and helping establish YWAM bases — from Denmark to Spain and Africa to Israel. They lived out of suitcases, witnessing on streets and beaches, and at cafes, universities, U.S. military installations, coffee houses and Bible studies. They also took the opportunity to study apologetics under the late Francis Schaeffer at L'Abri Fellowship in Huemoz, Switzerland. During their season with YWAM, Dennis and Ginger embraced God's call to a lifetime missions ministry.

When a call from Mom Lindsay brought the news of Gordon's

Dennis teaching Creation Science at CFNI

Dennis and Ginger with their three children—Missy, Hawni and Golan

The Dennis Lindsay Family

passing and a request for Dennis and Ginger to return to Dallas to assist her, they knew it was the time to become a part of Christ For The Nations. Dennis began teaching Bible classes, and until they started their family, Ginger taught Spanish.

Dennis and Ginger have three children. Their oldest, Missy Joy (23), is a CFNI graduate and a senior at Oral Roberts University, majoring in communications. Hawni Eve (21) is also a CFNI grad and is majoring in business administration at Dallas Baptist University. Golan Gordon (15) is a high school freshman.

During his 25 years at CFNI, Dennis has enjoyed teaching evangelism, apologetics, personal discipleship and Christian ethics. But he especially loves teaching creation science; he has written a dozen volumes in a projected 20-volume series on the subject. He has been invited to speak in churches and schools and he and Ginger have led outreaches and ministry teams. Over the years, they have ministered in 50 nations.

Ginger has become involved in ministry committees, teaching, and has developed and hosted CFN's annual International Women's Conference over the last seven years.

The Lindsays attend Oak Cliff Assembly of God, where Dennis has been a member since he was 5. He grew up under the dynamic ministry of the late Rev. H.C. Noah. Rev. Tom Wilson is now pastor.

As president and CEO, Dennis looks forward, together with Ginger, to continuing the vision of Gordon and Freda, expanding it as the Lord directs.

The First 25 Years

The Early Years of the Ministry

IT'S A PLEASURE FOR ME TO REFLECT UPON our early years. Though young and undiscerning then, I recall my parents' anticipation of a fresh move of the Spirit. From the pulpit and in his business contacts, my dad, Jack Moore, would say that as man's atomic power-bombs had shocked the world, ending World War II, he believed God was planning to show His power, and would have us involved.

God did. And THE VOICE OF HEALING was launched at the onset of that new wave of revival. It has become a flagship of balance through the ensuing decades, with revival's ebb and flow, and now rolling on into another millennium under its broader insignia: CHRIST FOR THE NATIONS. Initiated through the vision and teamwork of Gordon Lindsay and Jack Moore in 1948, over the years it became a major spiritual network under the continuing able leadership of the Lindsays.

At the same hour on God's prophetic clock, Israel

At work in
The Voice of Healing office in 1950

was reborn as a nation. His timing was evident in the birthing. The two newborns came forth bearing genetic imprints traceable to prophets of old. As surely as the ghostly handwriting on the palace wall at Belshazzar's midnight party brought a prophetic message, so through Israel's rebirth as a nation, a message was resonating to 20th-century Christendom: "The Final Countdown Has Begun!" The pen of an anointed scribe was positioned to begin writing ... "for such a time as this." The published page yet speaks ... in many lands and languages.

As we respect the acts of the Holy Spirit through all these years, our CFN archives have been carefully maintained. So from these, plus the wells of memory from which Freda Lindsay and I can draw deeply, comes this abbreviated review of a half-century faith-journey, the ripples of which have encircled the globe.

It has been quite a trip! Neither Freda nor I can say our schooling prepared us for such

challenges. Remember, though, that the Titanic was built by experts, but the Ark was built by amateurs ... who had heard from God!

(Note: Should the reader detect a nostalgic flashback — perhaps of sitting under a big tent, swept off our feet by an awesome Presence, hearts awash with cleansing tears that just keep coming — with every verse of "I'd Rather Have Jesus" — you needn't feel sorry for us. It was probably part of our conditioning for the marathon ahead, which, by the way, we're still running!)

— *Anna Jeanne Price*

"He has made His wonderful works to be remembered" (Psa. 111:4).

The Voice of Healing
A MONTHLY INTER-EVANGELICAL PUBLICATION OF THE LAST-DAY SIGN-GIFT MINISTRIES
BOX 4097
SHREVEPORT, LOUISIANA

SUBSCRIPTION RATE $1.00 PER YEAR

REV. GORDON LINDSAY
EDITOR

REV. JACK MOORE
CO-EDITOR

MISS ANNA JEANNE MOORE
MANAGING EDITOR

Dear Brother in Christ:

Please accept this complimentary issue of THE VOICE OF HEALING. Perhaps you are already one of the rapidly growing family of readers who subscribe to this new magazine. If so, we would appreciate it if you pass this copy on to someone else who you think would be interested. If you are not a subscriber we believe you will want to acquaint yourself with this publication.

THE VOICE OF HEALING, from the many reports that we are receiving, is filling a very definite spiritual need. It is inter-evangelical in scope, and is reporting the marvelous things that God is doing through the great sign-gift ministries that are now being manifested throughout the world. In seven months time the magazine achieved a circulation of 28,000, with subscriptions coming in, we confess, at a rate beyond our fondest expectations. No religious publication enjoys such a growth as this without some unique merit. We are glad for this great interest and intend to continue the policy that has been responsible for its rapid growth, namely:

1. To report the great sign-gift ministries that God is now giving to His church.

2. To encourage and further the unification of God's people in the closing hours of this age, especially in the bringing about of great united efforts of mass evangelism through the manifestation of the power of God.

3. To establish character to these efforts by advocating sound teaching, deep spirituality, and humility of all those associated in the great move of the Spirit of God.

4. To carry the outstanding faith-building messages of noted men of God.

5. To report the remarkable testimonials of healing and deliverance taking place currently.

6. To report, also, the latest prophetic developments as they point to the soon coming of Christ.

We believe you will want to fill out the subscription blank below, and, enclosing $1, you will receive the next copy of THE VOICE OF HEALING as it comes off the press.

Yours in His Glorious Service

Gordon Lindsay

GORDON LINDSAY
Editor

TULSA—JACK COE

Aristocratic Tulsa saw the largest gospel tent ever constructed, filled and overflowing as the healing ministry of Jack Coe of Fort Worth brought from 4,000 to 10,000 people nightly during his recent revival. At this writing the tent is up near Longview, Texas, and a good meeting is underway.

SALVATION DIVINE HEALING REVIVAL
Evangelist ... GAYLE JACKSON

PHOTO BY HARVEY PATTESON & SON

SAN ANTONIO — GAYLE JACKSON

All reports of this 8-week evangelistic endeavor by Evangelist Jackson and a number of Full Gospel pastors in S.A. describe it as "the greatest thing ever to hit S.A." Thousands saved and healed, and several hundred baptized with the Holy Ghost.

Throngs Gather In
Four of America's Largest Centers
NEW YORK · KANSAS CITY · SAN ANTONIO · TULSA

Attracted By the Ministry of

DIVINE HEALING

THOUSANDS OF CONVERSIONS TO CHRIST RECORDED

KANSAS CITY — WILLIAM BRANHAM

Associates of Brother Branham declared this to be "his best meeting yet." The miraculous was the ordinary. Full report in October TVH by cooperating pastor U.S. Grant.

NEW YORK CITY — T.L. OSBORN

At 5:30 on the morning of Sept. 9, long lines were formed around the St. Nicholas Arena awaiting the opening of one-day services among Spanish people. During the three services of that day, more outstanding miracles and healings took place than can be recorded, as witnessed by the crowd of over 7,000 (see page 15 in October TVH).

Simple Multiplication

The LORD your God has multiplied you, and here you are today... .

Deut. 1:10

It was God's idea. He said "be fruitful and multiply," and all nature heard and responded. Jesus' maxim on multiplying was "go and make disciples and teach." Gordon and Freda Lindsay heard, and began establishing Bible schools ... the very reason we're celebrating 50 fantastic years instead of only 25!

But first, let's go back to the starting line. Multiplication begins with two figures. We'll look in on two men, positioned by divine design, as the purveyors of this special God-project. Be my guest on this journey to the past; I was an eyewitness.

IN THE BEGINNING ... GOD

A better opening line could not be found for our story than that which opens HIS. And if there was any doubt that God was in the beginning of this Voice of Healing ministry, it was dissolved by mid-1948.

That would have been about the time of the first big hurdle, when the humble Baptist minister God used to inspire its inception collapsed from the exhaustion of continuous meetings and long prayer lines of suffering people, and asked to take leave from the ministry.

This meant that the Branham campaign schedules, made known to thousands of anxious subscribers through the new VOICE OF HEALING publications, must be canceled. The stirring revival reports and miraculous testimonies would not be forthcoming as promised, nor would there be crowds filling the large tents and auditoriums to hear and see the Gospel preached with signs following.

Gordon Lindsay and Jack Moore, those two figures pressed under the heavy responsibility in that crisis, began making 9-1-1 calls to heaven!

The Lord was there. He had not taken leave. Shutting down a mighty revival was never His aim. MULTIPLYING it was!

But His two special-assignment apostles didn't know that, so there was more waiting ... asking ... praying ... fasting. One thing Jack did know: He'd felt a prophetic prompting two years earlier to get ready to publish, and he'd obeyed.

So it was heaven's call now.

(Note: Our Father must enjoy seeing His children wait. It means that out on the road of life they can run and not be weary, walk and not faint. And a long, unpaved road lay ahead for these two and their wives, sons and daughters.)

THE 9-12 CALL

At last ... a direct call! A 9-12 call this time! Clear and credible: *"Turn you to the strong hold, ye prisoners of hope: even today do I declare that I will*

These four ministers met for the first time when Oral Roberts visited the Branham campaign in Kansas City, 1948. Left to right: Jack Moore, William Branham, Oral Roberts, Gordon Lindsay. A lasting bond of respect and common interests resulted from a time of prayer and discussion. Lindsay later wrote: "It appears evident that a unique ministry of healing is being manifested through Bro. Oral Roberts." Dr. Edwin Harrell, author of "All Things Are Possible," refers to Branham and Roberts as the "two giants of the healing revival."

render double unto thee" (Zech. 9:12 KJV).

They heard. They saw. It began to happen. While one ministry was down for R&R, two more were raised up. Subscriptions doubled. Instead of wanting their dollar back, subscribers were sending two, to pay for the next year, should we last that long! Churches ordered rolls of the power-packed magazines. Faith increased, and evangelists ordered new tents twice the size of their last one. The VOH staff doubled again and again, and the Moore Co. cleared another warehouse to accommodate the increasing work load. The largest post office box couldn't contain all the mail pouring in from the United States and overseas, requesting magazines, Bibles, anointed cloths, records, and ministers to come to their area.

It soon became evident that the Shreveport group were not the only ones hearing that call. Without long distance carriers, web sites, or e-mail, the Holy Spirit transmitted it far and near, to men with ears to hear and unknown names like Oral, T.L., Gayle, O.L., Tommy, Jack, Rudy, James, William, David, Burton, Abe, Velmer, Joseph, Walter, Wilbur, Louis, Paul, Dale, Doyle, Richard, Russ, Robert, Roy, F.F., L.D., A.A, W.V., Lester, Morris, Clif, Stan, Phil, Clair, Michael, Franklin, R.W., A.C., W.B., Kenneth, Gerald, Thelma, Louise, Fern, John, Olive, U.S., E.R., H.E., Al, Sam and MORE ... including names you can't pronounce, in places you can't find on your maps.

What on earth was going on in heaven? While worried atomic physicists went underground, pushing an arms race toward the first H-bomb that could rain more hellish terror than the A-bomb that just ended the worst of wars, *a stream of healing balm* from heaven was falling upon waiting, wonder-struck crowds in big city auditoriums and countryside camp meetings. It was awesome!

THE WORLD WAS GETTING A WAKE-UP CALL and none understood it better than men and women of the Word whose eyes had been on ISRAEL and who knew the signs of the seasons for which to watch.

HISTORIC CONVENTION OF TVH FELLOWSHIP GREAT SUCCESS (December '51) — Tulsa's Convention Hall Packed. Fourteen Full Gospel organizations represented — evangelists and editors in the foreground.

One of those unknown watchmen was a writer whose significant role in 20th-century Church history was aptly projected upon the scene for that momentous time. After centuries of painful, abortive thrashing about in the womb of the world, little Israel was birthed into the family of modern nations! And as Old Testament prophecies became headlines, the pen of that ready writer moved quickly to bring clarity to world events in the light of Bible prophecy. His Messianic tone, and the fresh in-depth magazine articles and book titles such as *Bible Days Are Here Again* and *Men Who Heard From Heaven,* brought the name of Gordon Lindsay out of obscurity for posterity.

In these early stages of this strategic ministry, Gordon could have sat back and enjoyed the fruit of his labor thus far. But neither he nor the incredible leading lady he had at his side had started on the goals they would reach in the years ahead.

And that's the *rest* of the story! An epic you don't want to miss. Their columns add up to staggering totals of literature printed, churches built, schools established, students trained, victims aided, and more ... still multiplying!

Since a drop of ink might make a million think, Jack and Gordon began publishing to influence *what* readers would think. And they succeeded.

And just as one drop of rain may start a flood — or one boy's lunch may feed a crowd —or one printed page may convert a tribe, so God's principles of multiplication never cease.

"Blessed is the man ... like a tree planted by streams of water, which yields its fruit in season and whose leaf does not wither. Whatever he does prospers. ... For the LORD watches over the way of the righteous" (Psa. 1:1,3,6 NIV).

A CONVENTION WITH A SIGNIFICANT VOICE

By DAVID J. DU PLESSIS
Secretary, WORLD PENTECOSTAL FELLOWSHIP

"There are... many kinds of voices in the world, and none of them is without signification." I Cor. 14-10.

Executives, pastors, evangelists, teachers and a host of witnesses enjoyed a time of wonderful spiritual fellowship during the VOICE OF HEALING CONVENTION. They were there from almost every state and from neighboring countries. "The Lord gave the word: great was the company of those that published it." Psa. 68:11. One of the constant highlights in many meetings was the testimony of those who had been perfectly healed of incurable diseases many years ago and have never lost their healing. Many were residents of Tulsa who were healed and saved in the great meetings of Raymond T. Richey in 1923 and later years. Scores of witnesses declared that they have an experimental knowledge of the healing power of God. Indeed, Divine Healing was presented with no uncertain voice by preaching and by witnessing, and the saints were also thrilled by the glorious presence of the Holy Spirit who confirmed the Word by the gifts and with signs following, as leading evangelists and teachers associated with "The Voice of Healing," brought soul-stirring messages from the Word of God.

"It is later than you think," was the theme of a message delivered by Oral Roberts. Not one who listened to him could have any doubt about the fact that we are living in momentous days, and that this is the time when God is "making bare His holy arm in the eyes of all the nations; and all the ends of the earth shall see the salvation of our God." Isa. 52:10. It is not possible that God should fail His people in this hour. Things that are happening in the world today do not come by accident. God's clock is just ticking off the moments which speedily bring us to the end of the age.

Several denominational preachers came to seek the Baptism and left rejoicing with the fullness of the Holy Ghost in their hearts. Pastors testified that they had been greatly encouraged and their vision had been enlarged by attending the conference. In the closing meeting there were over 500 pastors from more than a dozen Pentecostal Movements.

GORDON LINDSAY'S opening remarks emphasized that the purpose of this assemblage was not to form another organization, or to discount existing organizations, or to fuse them, but to be a liaison between all. He continued: "*When God was looking for a man to spear-head this revival, he didn't choose a brilliant man or a college professor who would be smart enough to start something for himself; He looked in the hills of Kentucky and found a humble, unassuming person, an uncolored type of John the Baptist, who in his simple, unlettered manner knew only to preach the Gospel and obey God's orders, seeking favor with no man. Our Brother Jack Moore found him, and recognizing the unusual anointing of God upon him, and feeling that he should not be restricted to any one group, flew to Oregon and let me in on this unique ministry.*

Bro. Jack Moore and I, though representing different groups, had been close friends for 18 years, often dreaming and talking of finding something that would be a touchstone for the unity of the widely-divided Pentecostal groups. We both recognized this to be what we had prayed for and set out to establish this Voice of Healing fellowship, beginning the magazine as a medium of publicizing the ministry."

Moved to Dallas in May 1952

Typical Testimonies and Quotes From the 50's and 60's

Summer of 1950 History-making Season for Evangelism

Jehovah's Witness Becomes Acts 1:8 Witness, Testimony of Charles Trombley

"Little David" Walker Conducting Campaigns Behind the Iron Curtain

T. Texas Tyler's Conversion - An Act of God

Student Converted Reading TVH in Hospital

E. R. Lindsay Sees Vision of Christ; Now Sees Thousands Receiving Salvation and Deliverance

Scars There, but T.B. Gone After Wearing Anointed Cloth

Healed of Goiter, Tumor, and Gall Bladder Ailments

Malignant Growth on Cheek Dissolves in Bandage After Prayer

Hearing In Right Ear First Time in 34 Years

Healed of Arthritis and Weak Eyes

Goiter Gone, Hearing Restored After 40 Years Deafness

Prayer Delivers From Multiple Sclerosis

Face Paralyzed, Speech Gone - Prayer Delivers

Ohio Woman Healed of Spinal Injury After Years in Brace

Healing From Rheumatic Fever Astounds Physician

Alcoholic Delivered

Cancer Disappears From Neck 10 Days After Anointed Cloth Received

Community Stirred by Healing of Hopeless Cancer Case

Crossed Eyes Straight

Delivered From Demon Possession

Pastor Healed of Curvature of the Spine

Lady walks after 18 years

Misplaced Vertebrae Straightens

State-wide prayer brings rain in Arizona

Hong Kong Sees Great Visitation in Culpepper Campaign

Circus "Fat Lady" - From 500 Pounds to 126
- McKay Ministry

2,000 attend Dale Hanson Revival in Toronto's Evangel Temple

Famous English Actor Becomes Evangelist
(from Freda Lindsay's interview with John French)

A Time-Tested Healing from B. D. Bennett Campaign Legs crushed, Man Walks Out Minus Crutches

Louise Nankivell Meetings Blessing Thousands "Small Woman in Sackcloth with Unique Sign-Gifts"

"No Man Has Been a Greater Blessing to TVH than the Well-Known Evangelist, W. V. Grant, Sr."
- Gordon Lindsay '58

Don Price, Apostle To Thailand No Longer With us But His Work Marches On

"John the Baptist" Osteen Greatly Used of God

Crooked Foot and Leg Instantly Straight as Olive Kellner Prays

Supernatural Accompanies Paul Cain Ministry

"Baffling Boy Sees, Reads With Plastic Eye; Optometrist agrees It's God's Gift" - The Chattanooga News

Pastor Sends Remarkable Testimonies After 7-week Revival with Evang. James Drush

"Healing Campaigns are Worthwhile" According to Survey by Evang. W. A. Henry

"William Branham as I Knew Him"
(Editor Reviews the incomparable ministry of his esteemed co-minister following auto crash that took his life.) Feb. 1966 issue

TVH's Winning The Nations Crusade Helps Conserve Fruit in El Salvador and Korea

---

EDITOR LEAVES THE FIELD TO DEVOTE HIMSELF TO THE MAGAZINE

Because of the vast responsibility of carrying on the work of THE VOICE OF HEALING, the editor has decided not to engage in any more campaigns on the field, until the Lord leads otherwise. The magazine this month has reached a circulation of nearly 80,000. To properly edit the magazine and superintend TVH publications, it is necessary for him to devote more time at the office in Shreveport. He does expect to be on the field part of the time, however.

THE MAGAZINE USED IN AMERICA'S GREAT HEALING REVIVALS

April-May

THE VOICE OF HEALING

SPECIAL THIRD
ANNIVERSARY
ISSUE

Circulation 75,000
Price 20c

World-Wide Revivals Continue

AT HOME
U. S. Congressman Walks Without
Crutches After 66 Years a Cripple

ABROAD
Salvation-Healing Meetings Influence
Thousands of Natives to Accept Christ

FROM THE DESK OF...
Anna Jeanne

I can't recall a testimony more impressive than Wm. Upshaw's. A fractured spine at 18 left him dependent on wheel chairs and crutches for life, but his famous slogan was _Never give up!_ His instant healing at 84 astonished thousands who had known him as a crippled congressman, presidential candidate, vice-president of the So. Baptist Convention, and educator. He finished out his life traveling in Europe and U.S. telling of his miracle, even going to the very spot in Washington where he had sat 8 years in Congress and standing whole among them gave his verbal, visible witness to the healing power of Jesus Christ! (Personal note: At our wedding he steadily walked me down Westminster's aisle to Don Price, then excused himself to rush over to London's Trafalgar Square to testify, walk and talk among the Saturday afternoon crowd!)

Sampling of TVH Headlines Helps Describe Events of the Early Years

The truth about the present move of God in the historic churches

The Voice of Healing Mount of Olives Chapel becomes a reality

Father-Son team, Al & Tommy Reid, conduct great campaigns in the Philippines – founding 17 outstations

Revival spirit continues in Fort Worth church after Hagin revival closes ('54)

India thousands witness mighty move of God as the M.A. Daouds minister to 60,000

Kansas City Times gives fine report of Branham meeting, Pensacola stirred for God under Branham party

Editor resigns church at Ashland, Oregon

Oral Roberts present at Kansas City campaign

Jewish evangelists Kaplan and Tannenbaum having unusual healings

Thousands of Texans flock to Jack Coe tent

Mighty stir in New Orleans as 5,586 saved in Gayle Jackson revival

Miracles "en Masse"... 50,000 confess Christ in Cuba (Osborns)

Raymond T. Richey joins The Voice of Healing

Billy Graham in Shreveport; commends The Voice of Healing

Tommy Hicks draws largest crowd in Gospel history – 400,000; commended by Argentine President Peron

Morris Cerullo's ministry reaching thousands in America and abroad

25,000 respond to altar call in David Nunn Mexico City meetings; 79,000 in Puerto Rico

Strongholds crumble in San Salvador (Evang. Richard Jeffery)

Crowds of 50,000 hear Erickson in Brazil

Prices see first outpouring in Thailand

Revival sweeps Greenville under ministry of James Dunn

3,000 fill tent to hear Velmer Gardner in Clarksburg, W. VA.

Sam Todd's greatest victory is in Seoul, Korea: The Voice of Healing helps fund first building, (point of origin of world's largest church.)

How a Reformed Church minister received the Pentecostal experience – by Harald Bredesen

The amazing conversion of leading atheist Ralph Underwood

Outlawing of prayer in public schools a national disaster

Born again in Osborn-Lindsay campaign, Mennonite Gerald Derstine begins effective ministry

"One of the greatest ever," Pastor says about Grant's Bastrop Revival

Outstanding deliverances as L. D. Hall ministers

Pastor Sumrall's prayer delivers girl from demons
(Manila newspaper)

Boy blind since infancy healed in Kronberg revival

Tumors disappear in Ralph Durham tent meeting

Phoenix Pastor reports outstanding healings in deliverance revival with John Poteet

AG minister delivered of 30-pound tumor after prayer in H.E. Hardt ministry

Leper completely well two weeks after Osborn's Java crusades

Elmira heights blessed under powerful De Grado ministry

The Voice of Healing reports greatest foreign revivals in history of the world

Stroudsburg, PA stirred by L.C. Robie Campaign

Glorious report of Ogilvie campaigns

Richard Nixon at Full Gospel Business Men's Convention

"Bible deliverance built my Church"...Pastor H. P. Vibbert

Liberal, KS area stirred by A.S. Teuber revival; many outstanding testimonies of healing

12,000 attend Rudy Cerullo campaign in Cuba (1954)

Osborn World Missions Crusade evangelizes through the natives

Ceylon shaken by the power of God as A.C. Valdez, Jr. ministers

A call to the business men of our nation
by Demos Shakarian

It is inspiring to see a godly heritage, a ministry, or talent repeated in a succeeding generation. For example, Billy Graham / Franklin; Pat Robertson / Gordon; Gordon Lindsay / Dennis; Tommy Barnett / Matt; F.F. Bosworth / Bob; Oral Roberts / Richard; Al Reid / Tommy; Jack Coe / Jack Jr.; Wayne Myers / David; Randy Delp / Kevin; Duane Weis / Bob; Jack Hatcher / John; Carroll Thompson / Victor; Dan Marocco / Jim; Bert Allbritton / David; Tom Wilson / Scott; Rodney Duron / Denny; Gerald Mangun / Anthony; Charles Green / Michael; Kenneth Hagin / Ken; Lester Sumrall / Steve; John Meares / Don; Roland Gardner / Landy… and others.

Allow us a personal reference to two smiling young men standing together in the group pictured. (Center, back row.) Clair Hutchins and Don Price, TVH evangelists, both having come from professional music careers, devoted their lives to preaching the Gospel. Away on missions together they prayed for their children and talked of their future. Both have gone to their reward, but each has a daughter blessing many with anointed music.

Typical of the shift of emphasis from healing campaigns to world evangelization, this group of ministers from varied organizations met in Dallas to explore the possibilities of world missions. Seated: (l to r) Dr. Clyde Belin, John Douglas, David J. duPlessis, J. Mattson Boze, Mrs. Jack Coe, L.S. Heaston, Gordon Lindsay. Standing middle: (l to r) Maxwell Whyte, Carlton Spencer, Harry Hampel, R.C. Cook, Carmine DiBiase, Leon Hall. Back Row (l to r) J.E. Wilson, Cecil Truesdale, Walter Gravlin, Clair Hutchins, Don Price, J.M. Sickler, Jack Moore, John Meares.

Carol Hutchins Cymbala is the director of the great BROOKLYN TABERNACLE CHOIR, known to millions. Jodie Price Aaron began at 15 to lead the Life Tabernacle Singers, influencing southern churches and CFN music in the '70s. What a joy to parents' hearts are faithful children. And who could deny that anointed music can be a means of multiplication. Jim Cymbala started with 20 people, and is planning now to acquire space for 4,000 in Brooklyn, N.Y.

Jodie Aaron

Carol Cymbala and the Brooklyn Tabernacle Choir

REVIVAL SPREADS TO DISTANT SHORES

Above: Ponce, Puerto Rico – one of Osborn's first massive overseas crusades.
Below: Sam Todd sent by God to Korea; results still multiplying as world's largest church continues to grow.
At Bottom: Tommy Hicks' historic campaign in Argentina draws up to 400,000

Moving with the Ebb and Flow of God's Spirit

At Left: Gordon and Freda on location with daughter, Shira, as she makes a film about Israel. Above: Gordon pointing to the Mount of Olives Chapel built by the Voice of Healing ministry.

In the late '50s and early '60s, Gordon Lindsay observed that the extraordinary wave of God's healing power was beginning to ebb. It was time to seek God for new direction, new vision. And God gave it to him. One of his primary burdens was for the people of the land of Israel.

In 1952, Gordon took his first trip to Israel along with several ministers. But it was seven years later that God divinely sent him back to set in motion a plan to reach the Jews. It was time for the "dry bones" to arise! He saw that the "church" approach didn't work in Israel, proof of which were the few tiny churches with a handful of attendees. The people of Israel need to meet, once again, the God of miracles through the Messiah.

Having arrived in Israel for an exploratory tour, Gordon was wishing he had someone with him to take pictures. As he stepped into the elevator at the YMCA in Jerusalem, whom should he meet but evangelist Paul Kopp — a million-to-one chance? Gordon knew Paul's preacher father. So the two rented a car and covered the land from Dan to Beersheba, Paul using his movie camera. Note: later that year, Paul moved his entire family to Jerusalem, including his son Charles, who is still there today. Then on one of our first Israel tours, Elizabeth, a lovely young lady whose parents pastored in Chicago, accompanied us. In Tiberias, we introduced her to Charles, by now a handsome young man in his twenties and over six feet tall. A year later, they married and today have seven fine Christian children — the oldest two of whom are CFNI graduates.

Gordon Lindsay

Native Church Program Initiated

CFN's first Native Church project (1961)

CFN's 10,000th Native Church project (1997)

The Lord had been speaking to Gordon Lindsay's heart for a whole year about building churches. In 1961, the Lindsays and several others took a missionary trip throughout Central and South America, where they saw firsthand the need for more church buildings. Just after that trip, Freda's niece and her husband, Herman and Viola Engelgau, who had served as missionaries in Africa for many years, told Gordon, "There are so many towns and villages that need churches. With just $250, they could purchase the materials to build a church."

Gordon instantly recognized that was the plan, and the vision began to unfold. Through supporters, the ministry would supply missionaries with the funds for materials (roofing, windows, doors, etc.) to help congregations finish the construction of their buildings. The congregation would be responsible to purchase the land and provide the labor. Since 1961, CFN's Native Church program has helped more than 10,000 Third-World congregations complete their facilities.

"The Native Church program is a simple plan by which any American family can sponsor the building of a native church in a foreign missionary field and thus have a vital part in fulfilling Christ's command to evangelize the nations."

*— **Gordon Lindsay***

Wayne Myers is a long-time friend

A celebration of 50 years of ministry

A Missionary Statesman

Wayne Myers became a part of God's kingdom at age 14. He was filled with the Spirit and called to preach while serving in the Pacific aboard the USS Enterprise during World War II.

Wayne has spent the following 50 years taking the love of Christ to Mexico and over 70 nations on every continent.

Wayne is known for the lifestyle and message of "Living to Give," and as the "missionary of missionaries." He considers himself a "general practitioner" and goes where God calls him and does whatever is asked of him. He is at the top of the list of favorite guest speakers at Christ For The Nations Institute in Dallas.

One of the most outstanding facets of Wayne's ministry is as a missionary broker–assisting missionaries in many nations with financial help or equipment. Also, he has represented Christ For The Nations in Mexico as a Native Church supervisor since the inception of the program, which has helped roof over 3,500 churches in Mexico alone.

Altogether, Wayne, Martha and their three children and spouses have given over 150 years to world missions. One daughter and her husband are ministering in Spain, and their other daughter is married to a Christian surgeon. Their only son is on furlough after spending 15 years in Spain.

Wayne gives the devil a hard time just keeping up with him, and is a relentless, faithful and godly worker for the Lord.

Recipients of CFN's literature

The Christian Center

The New Vision Began Taking Shape

In 1965, the Literature Crusade program was initiated utilizing 13 of Gordon's books for adults and three books by other authors for children. Since that time, tens of millions of these books have been distributed free in Third-World nations.

In 1966, with their office/print shop being inadequate, the Lindsays put a down payment on several lots located just seven miles from downtown Dallas on which they would construct a new headquarters building.

Soon after, they discovered that adjacent to their property there was a bankrupt nightclub for sale. Through a miraculous chain of events, that building was secured and became The Christian Center. The Lindsays began to hold seminars there several times a year. They invited leading Charismatic ministers such as Kenneth Hagin and John Osteen.

In May of 1967, some 19 years after The Voice of Healing was started, the new name Christ For The Nations was adopted to reflect the fact that the ministry was now worldwide in scope.

Headquarters groundbreaking

Headquarters – dedicated in 1969

In 1970, Gordon told Freda one day that he felt they should start a Bible school. Freda hesitated, feeling that was a work for a younger man, and reminded Gordon that he was in his mid-sixties and was already doing more than most for the Lord. The Lindsay's three children discouraged him from beginning such a project as well. But Gordon believed it was a mandate from God, and he persisted until he finally convinced Freda.

When they began to pray about teachers for the school, Freda had an idea. Since they could not afford a large faculty, why not bring in special guests for the last class each weekday morning. So when Christ For The Nations Institute opened that very fall with an enrollment of about 50, Gordon had appointed Dr. Marvin Solum as director and Rev. Leonard Ravenhill as the first resident faculty member. Various visiting ministers that year included Harald Bredesen, Derek Prince, Charles Duncombe, Kenneth Hagin, Loren Cunningham, John Osteen, Maxwell Whyte, Wayne Myers, Paul Paino and Joe Poppell. The first two years, classes were held in the Christian Center.

The original vision was for an intensive, nine-month course for ministers, missionaries, evangelists and laymen. The courses included Spiritual Gifts, Prophecy, The Book of Revelation, Ministry of the Supernatural, Bible Characters, Life of Christ, Personal Witnessing, Evangelism and Pastoring. In addition, the guest lecturers from all over the world spoke on various topics. There were special prayer sessions, and the students were encouraged to wait upon God.

Knowing they would need housing for the students as the school grew, the Lindsays went to work right away to have part of their land rezoned so they could build a dormitory. But the day after the zoning was granted, a gentleman came to them. He owned several apartment complexes and a restaurant right next to their property. He informed them that he had cancer and the doctor had given him only six months to live. He urged the Lindsays to buy his apartment complexes, and told them they would need only a small down payment on one of the complexes. That's how CFNI's first several dormitories were obtained.

CFNI's first student body and staff

*One of the four complexes
named Gospel Courts —
Matthew, Mark, Luke and John*

Mary Martha House

King's House

Viking

Air Force Chaplain Flies High

As a retired USAF chaplain, I had been ordained by my denomination for 17 years when we arrived at Torrejon AFB, Madrid, Spain in 1970. I was about as liberal a pastor as anyone could find. I tried to be with "the troops," but I had nothing to share with them. I was responsible for the 0900 Sunday service, which was small to non-existent. People seldom came back after their first visit.

Then something happened in the summer of 1972. The senior chaplain was on leave and I was sort of in charge of the Protestant work while he was gone. I got a series of phone calls from a group wanting to "help" us at the base. Among other things, they suggested a coffee house. The day the senior chaplain returned, he shared a letter with me from a chaplain friend in Germany telling him that if he did not have a YWAM (Youth With A Mission) team on his base, he should get one ASAP.

Good News! The group that had called were YWAMers! That's how I met Dennis and Ginger Lindsay and Dennis' older sister, Shira. I was impressed that Shira came from her work in Israel to submit herself to a YWAM team led by her youngest brother. Everything was soon cleared for a coffee house, with me assigned as "Project Officer." I quickly gained a whole new view of Christianity from those YWAMers, and we soon had revival at Torrejon AFB. The coffee house was filled every afternoon and evening. We had new commitments to the Lord happening daily. Our Sunday service attendance increased greatly, too.

Sondra and I saw real Christianity close up. Those YWAMers, led by Dennis, Ginger and Shira, lived their Christianity. They knew what Christ meant when He said "Go and make disciples." One other important part of this was that they prayed! Every day at the team's prayer time they prayed for us as a family and as individuals.

Sondra was the first one of our family to give her life to the Lord, only six days before she left with Dennis' team for the 1972 Munich Olympic Outreach. While they were in Munich, I prayed through with one of their team members — accepting Jesus as my Lord and Savior.

— *Phil and Sondra Hampe*

Gordon Goes To Heaven

The institute flourished under the Lindsays' leadership. The enrollment for spring semester of 1973 reached 250. At the CFNI service on Sunday, April 1, 1973, exactly on Gordon's 25th anniversary as president of the ministry, as Freda was at the podium making announcements, she became aware of the faculty walking around behind her. Before she even turned her head, she sensed the scurrying about had something to do with Gordon. When she looked around, there he sat with his head on his shoulder; as though he were asleep; but Gordon had gone to heaven while seated on the platform.

Gordon's funeral was a grand celebration. That afternoon as Charles Duncombe ministered to those gathered in the auditorium, a prophetic message came forth that this work had been founded on the Rock Christ Jesus and would continue more gloriously than in the past. And it has.

The Call of the Harvest
By Gordon Lindsay

The story of a young person called of God but who waited to respond until it was too late.

Sunrise and skies are fair
A day begins without a care:
A day for joy, a day for leisure,
A day for thrills, a day for pleasure.
Youth is merry, youth is gay;
The great Grim Reaper is far away.

But there is a call; 'tis the Master's voice:
"I need you today; may I be your choice?
A harvest is waiting and fields are white,
Will you join the reapers in the morning bright?
Awake, O youth, to the heavenly vision:
Multitudes — multitudes in the valley of decision."

Morning sun, high above the earth;
A cry of distress in the midst of mirth.
Heathen are born and heathen die;
Is there none to hear their cry?
"Oh yes," said the youth, "count me as one,
To help in the harvest till the day is done."
(Yet he lingered on for a little more fun.)

High sun and high noon:
"You'll be hearing from me soon.
I've married a wife; I've property to see,
Five yoke of oxen acquired by me.
I'll soon heed to the call and join the band
Ready to give the reapers a hand."
(But he tarried on; he'd a bargain in land.)

Afternoon sun and afternoon light,
The golden orb hastened its flight.
Conscience still heard; memory daunted.

Gordon Lindsay— a valiant prayer warrior, a prolific writer, and a man with a vision for the world

Gordon in his beloved Israel

Paul Finkenbinder (Hermano Pablo) interviewing Gordon in El Salvador ('55)

Gordon and Loren Cunningham, founder of Youth With A Mission

Gordon and Freda presenting Madame Gandhi with a Bible and a check for the children who were India-Bangladesh war victims ('72)

Gordon in Kenya ('72)

Gordon — known affectionately to his family as "daddy"

Wealth he'd acquired, yet more was wanted.
(Many were the possessions he proudly flaunted.)

Houses and barns, lands and farms,
Streams and ponds, stocks and bonds,
Chickens and hogs, forest and logs,
Sheep and cows, thoroughbred sows,
Crops and flax, meadows and haystacks,
Orchards and cherries, vineyards and berries.

Day was waxing and day was waning,
Still the rich man was entertaining.
For a sinister voice had spoken and said,
"On with the fun; on with the dance;
Make merry while you have a chance.

You're a man of the times — ten feet tall."
To conscience he said, "Time yet for the call."
So a little more folly, and a little more fun.
(And the hours slipped away until there were none.)

Sun rise to sun fall;
The day was wasting on the western wall.
Hands still busy with a thousand things,
As evening descends and curfew rings.
The day has faded into twilight red,
As multitudes hastened to join the dead.

"I am ready; I am ready," said the man at last.
But shaking hands could not hold fast.
Hair unnoticed had turned to gray,
Still he thought it was yesterday.
Alas, harvest past, it was too late to save
Those who had gone to a Christless grave.

Where is the silver; where is the gold?
Where are the possessions to another sold?
Where are the sheep that grazed on the hill?
Where are the cattle that drank from the rill?
Where are the barns that were filled with plenty?
Where are the thoroughbreds, one-hundred and twenty?
Where are the heirlooms; where are the treasures?
Where is the laughter; where are the pleasures?
Where are the parties; where is the wine?
Where are the delicacies and dinners so fine?

Sun sunk low and night descending,
Summer is gone, and the harvest is ending.
Oh, for a chance for time extended.
(A wasted life was never intended.)

Sun fall and moon rise,
What is left of the rich man's prize?

Go out through the valley to yonder hill,
And see the marble standing still.
Treasures offered in heaven; but he took instead
The cold reward of the unsaved dead.

And what of us who live today?
This is our hour; let us not stay.
A call to the harvest till it shall end.
Work now, work fast, reap, my friend.

New dawn and sun rise,
To the faithful the Master will give the prize.

The Second 25 Years

THE DAY AFTER GORDON DIED, Freda received a phone call from Kenneth Hagin, a longtime friend of the family. His words brought encouragement to Freda's heart: "Great new doors of service are going to open to you. Don't be afraid."

Just one day following the funeral, the fulfillment of those words began: CFN's board voted Freda to succeed Gordon as president. The ministry flourished under Freda's leadership. Though she turned 84 in April of this year (1998), she still serves in an advisory capacity to her son, Dennis — Christ For The Nations' chairman of the board, president and CEO — and the ministry team he has established.

Freda visiting the needy in Ethiopia

Freda Lindsay greeting Pat Robertson after he spoke at a CFNI graduation banquet

Freda with Voice of Healing evangelists at 1986 reunion

Freda speaking at Washington For Jesus 1988

Freda dancing the Jewish hora with daughter and son-in-law, Shira and Ari Sorko-Ram

Freda enjoying Jerusalem on one of her many trips to Israel

Freda took up Gordon's mantle

Freda with managing director, Norman Young

The day after Gordon's funeral, CFN's 10-man board unanimously voted Freda to succeed Gordon as president of the ministry. The task seemed overwhelming to her, but with the prayers and encouragement of the board, staff and faculty, Freda forged ahead. She became known as "the widow who picked up the mantle."

Freda had always been adept at business matters, thus she was able to keep the ministry running smoothly after Gordon's passing. Actually, the ministry began expanding rapidly under her leadership, and perhaps due to sympathy felt by friends, she received unparalled financial support. Freda, since her Bible school days when she was challenged to read the Bible through completely once every year, has been a woman of the Word. "Three chapters a day, and five on Sunday," is her motto. And with Gordon's priority on prayer, she learned to be a woman of prayer as well. From CFNI's 1974 yearbook: "A pastor who knows Sister Lindsay calls her 'a precious woman of prayer.' A lawyer who knows her said, wiping his brow after a conference, 'That's the toughest little lady I've ever negotiated with.' Both evaluations are true."

By August of that year ('72), the Institute Building was completed and enrollment climbed to 425.

In 1974, CFN's bookstore opened — to serve the student body and the community

Gordon Lindsay Hall

Maranatha

A Season of "Firsts"

It was in 1974 that CFNI produced its first chorus tape, directed by praise and worship leader Bill Kaiser, who was assisted by David Myers. Since that time, CFNI has produced a praise and worship project every year, and in 1997 began to produce a second yearly project at the annual worship conference. Besides audio tapes, today CDs, videos and lead sheets are available.

The first CFNI summer outreach took place that year, with Dennis Lindsay leading the group to Mexico. That summer outreach program has become a hallmark of CFNI.

It offers students interested in missions the opportunity to experience other cultures and to use the ministry training they have received.

Between 1974 and 1976, several more apartment complexes for student housing were obtained. Also a motel was purchased, called Gordon Lindsay Hall. Its 80 rooms served as dorm rooms for single men, its banquet rooms were converted into classrooms and a prayer chapel, its spacious lobby was turned into registration offices, and its large restaurant was made the school cafeteria.

Agape House

The First CFNI outreach team

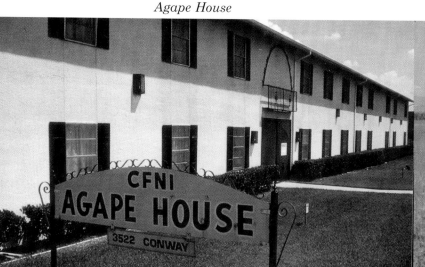

Bob and Emma Humburg poured their hearts into starting Glaubenszentrum

In 1976, Christ For The Nations experienced another first — a Bible school in Europe. When God began preparing to do a mighty work in Germany, He selected the Humburg family. Until he was 32 years of age, Bob lived a miserably hopeless life as a gambler, a bookmaker and an alcoholic. But through the faithful prayers of his wife, Emma, and at the invitation of a radio minister at 3 a.m. one morning, he surrendered his life to Jesus. Eight years later, Bob sold his small business and moved his entire family to Dallas to attend CFNI. In time, the entire family graduated, and all four children met their future spouses while attending.

While they were at CFNI, the Lord gave Bob and Emma a burden for Germany. Two of their girls, Kay and Lynn, and another Kay, spent 15 months in Germany, praying for a Bible school. God answered prayer. Bob found a huge structure for sale in Wolfenbuttel; it had been built by Hitler to train his troops, and Glaubenszentrum (Faith Center) started in 1976.

When the enrollment for the school kept growing, God provided another Hitler-built facility in Bad Gandersheim. Two years ago, to accommodate the month-end conferences, a nearby hotel was purchased. This year, a beautiful, 1,000-seat auditorium was built on the school property. Today, Mike and Kay (Humburg) Chance direct the growing Bible school and the entire operation. To God be the glory!

Mike and Kay (Humburg) Chance direct Glaubenszentrum today

A Good Problem —
Too Many Students!

Dayspring (Morning Star's behind it)

The Music Building

Bethel

In 1976, with the student enrollment at 1,000, the institute was bursting at the seams. Two huge apartment complexes were purchased that year —Colonial Gardens Apartments, later named Dayspring and Morning Star — to accommodate the needs of family housing.

Music had become an integral part of the institute, and space was needed for offices, practice rooms, etc. So another small building was purchased, and later added onto — the Music Building.

More space was needed for classrooms and offices and nurseries... so plans were made to build a huge Student Center. That beautiful building was completed in 1977.

Before and after the institute auditorium expansion

With so many students, now the institute auditorium simply wasn't big enough. That expansion project was finished in 1979, with the auditorium seating 2,200. And since additional housing was needed again, another apartment complex was purchased and named Bethel.

The Student Center

The Jerusalem Center

I n 1980, CFN bought a lovely four-story building, which is called the Jerusalem Center. The first floor is used as a chapel by Jews, Arabs and American tour groups. The second floor provides a home for the faithful overseers, Charles and Elizabeth Kopp, and their lovely family. The third story and the daylight basement are used primarily for guests.

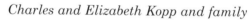

Charles and Elizabeth Kopp and family

The Jack Moore Library Chapel

For any thriving school, a good library is a must. The Jack Moore Library Chapel, which was dedicated in 1982, not only contains an excellent library, but office space, prayer rooms and a beautiful chapel that doubles as a classroom.

That year, the well-known refugees, the Siberian Seven arrived in Dallas after a prolonged and difficult effort to have them released. That group was the first of several from Russia and Eastern Europe that CFN sponsored.

Having snatched up all the available apartments nearby, and still needing more housing for the growing student body, the Cornerstone apartments were built in 1983.

The Siberian Seven

Cornerstone

A Time of Honor for Freda

Dr. McPherson bestowing Freda's first honorary doctorate

Dr. Oral Roberts conferring an honorary doctorate of Humane Letters

A Time of Honor for Freda Lindsay's first honorary doctorate was bestowed by the son of the founder of the Foursquare Church, Dr. Rolph McPherson. The doctorate of divinity was given to her on May 29, 1977 at the International Foursquare Convention in Portland, Oregon. Her second honorary doctorate — a doctorate of Humane Letters — was bestowed at the Oral Roberts University May 2, 1987 by Dr. Oral Roberts. Then on June 20, 1983, over 200 people turned out to honor Freda as Christian Woman of the Year at an elegant awards ceremony held at the North Dallas home of Clint and Anne Murchison. (Clint was then owner of the Dallas Cowboys, and Anne a Christian author and lecturer.) The award was sponsored by five Christian organizations. The evening's festivities were filmed by the 700 Club, Dallas newspapers covered the event, *Charisma* and *Christian Life* magazine ran stories about Freda and the awards ceremony.

Dr. Cory SerVaas, editor and publisher of "The Saturday Evening Post", read the proclamation.

Mrs. Anne Murchison, author and lecturer, presented Freda with a beautiful gold trophy.

Robert Walker, editor of "Christian Life" magazine, gave Freda a plaque.

Ken and Gloria Copeland

Gerald and Beulah Derstine

Dr. Bill and Vonette Bright

The guest list at the Christian Woman of the Year awards ceremony could have well been labeled "Who's Who in the Ministry."

The head table — with (L to R) Dr. & Mrs. Robert Walker, Dr. Cory SerVaas, Dr. Freda Lindsay, George Otis, Anne Murchison and Stephen Strang, editor of Charisma

Stephen Strang prayed for Freda

Rev. and Mrs. Dick Mills

John and Joy Dawson, George Otis

Jim and Nancy Spillman

Before and after CFN puchased this building for the men's dorm and school cafeteria

The mid '80s brought more growth and a shift in the leadership. CFN started its first branch school in 1983 — Christ For The Nations Institute of Biblical Studies in beautiful Stony Brook, New York. The school effectively served the northeast region of the United States until 1991. Since the cafeteria and the dorm rooms in Gordon Lindsay Hall (GLH) were far too cramped, Freda jumped at the chance to purchase the 10-story Sheraton when it went up for sale.

Dennis Lindsay became CFN's president in '85; Freda remained chairman of the board until '94

GLH was used as a down payment for the building. The facility stands as a landmark between two busy freeways. In 1985, Freda, being 71 years old, resigned from the position of president, though she remained CEO and chairman of the board for some years. The Lindsay's youngest son, Dennis, who had served faithfully on the faculty since his father's homegoing, was voted by the board to be president.

CFN's Institute of Biblical Studies — Stony Brook, NY

Caribbean CFNI's first building

Director Peter Burnett
and his wife, Betty

God Leads to a Nightclub

In 1986, Christ For the Nations was praying for just the right location for a Bible school in the Caribbean. But where? Haiti? The Dallas graduates desiring missions training would first need to learn French. Puerto Rico? They'd need to learn Spanish. Then why not Jamaica, where they could speak English and begin ministering immediately?

So the search began for a building there. God led Norman Young and Mark Ott, CFNI staff members, to a bankrupt nightclub in Montego Bay. Located only a few miles from the airport, the building sat on an 11-acre tract overlooking the Caribbean Sea - a breathtaking view.

A team was formed and renovation began on the buildings. Students came from all over the Caribbean to attend the Bible school. One beautiful dormitory was built, then a second, and later a third. A magnificent 800-seat auditorium was also constructed. Experienced teachers from Dallas have served as directors of Caribbean Christ For the Nations, including Randy Delp, Hilton Mansfield, Bruce Vernon and Peter Burnett, all of whom are also CFNI graduates. Other CFNI alumni teach and labor, supported by friends' donations.

The campus is also used year-round by groups coming from the U.S. and Canada - for youth groups to get involved in missions, for pastors' conferences, and for a CFNI seminar each January. It's also a beautiful vacation spot for Christians to seek God and get a little R & R.

The enlarged campus

Director George Carothers with wife Emilie and three sons

Our Judeas and Samarias

For 19 years, since Christ For the Nations Institute was opened in Dallas, some of the Canadian students prayed that a CFNI would be opened in their land. A large number of Canadians attended CFNI in Dallas; however, only the more affluent could attend, since they are not permitted to work in the U.S. On the other hand 85 - 90% of Americans work at least part of their way through college. CFNI scholarships are granted yearly to 200-300 students, yet they are mainly granted to those from Third-World nations. (Even so, hundreds of Canadians are rejected each semester.)

In 1989, the search for a facility led to Vancouver, B.C., to a former funeral home being rented by The Centre of Positive Living. The price was negotiated, but the group requested a six-month partial occupancy. However, through prayer, they vacated in a few days. A four-plex was later purchased and dedicated in the fall of 1997.

After several years, the school was not large enough. So a beautiful and much larger, unfinished church was purchased and dedicated in the fall of 1997.

Directors of the school, Rev. George and Emily Carothers, are both graduates from CFNI-Dallas. They met on campus, and now have three beautiful sons. Many of the graduates from CFNI-Canada are in full-time ministry, reaching not only the Canadians, but the multitudes of Asians who fled the takeover of Hong Kong, bringing their wealth and their heathen gods. Every summer, while the school's annual summer student outreaches to Asia touch many lives, their excellent choir tours the Canadian provinces.

CFNI Canada's first building

CFNI Canada's new facility

Youth For The Nations

John Collins and wife, Joann
Director of Youth Ministries

Brad and Denise Howard
Founding Directors of YFN

The first Youth For the Nations was held in 1989. The purpose of the program is two-fold: 1) to minister to this generation of youth, inspiring them to commit to a life-long dedication to the Lord, and 2) to offer hands-on experience to CFNI youth ministers in training.

The founding directors were Brad and Denise Howard, CFNI graduates now pastoring a church near Dallas. Presently, the program is overseen by the director of youth ministries, John Collins. This life-transforming youth camp has impacted the lives of thousands of young people.

Thousands of young people
attend YFN every year

YFN activities —
geared for the youth
culture

Amidst all the fun, lives are radically changed for Christ.

Romania — Big Returns

Seven of the fine Romanians hand-picked by John Dolinschi to be trained at CFNI-Dallas

John Dolinschi climbed the mountains of Eastern Europe to make his escape from Communist Romania. In America, John worked and saved his money to study at Christ For the Nations Institute-Dallas, where he graduated from in 1986. Several times, he secretly returned to Romania, bearing Bibles and preaching in underground churches.

When the Communist dictator Ceausescu and his wife were killed on Christmas Day 1989, John quickly made his plans. He prayerfully and carefully selected several young Christian students and urged CFN to give them one year of free schooling. Most were married and had to leave their wives and children behind. These dedicated believers returned to Romania at the end of their year. Then they requested financial help to start two Bible schools at opposite ends of their country - one in Timisoara and one in Suceava – to train church leaders for its population of 23 million.

CFN hosted a small tour group of missions-minded Americans to Eastern Europe, including a retired couple from Washington, Stan and Helen Walters. (Stan had been a businessman who had owned a heavy construction equipment plant.) The Walters helped purchase the land for both schools, later adding considerable gifts to help other CFN donors build those two beautiful schools. Hundreds of students have already been trained there to pastor, teach, and lead worship.

Rev. and Mrs. Walter Kronberg, long-time friends of CFN, shipped their huge gospel tent to Romania. With the graduates helping Kronberg, churches were planted in every city in which he preached, resulting in a bountiful harvest of souls and supplying additional students for the two schools. Praise God.

CFNI in Suceava, Romania, which was started in 1991

CFNI in Timisoara, Romania, which began in 1992

International Women's Conference

I n 1991, Ginger Lindsay, wife of President Dennis Lindsay, instituted an annual international women's conference. The conference has grown over the years, and is now one of CFN's largest special events.

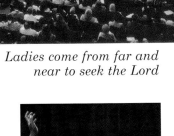

Ladies come from far and near to seek the Lord

Hostess Ginger Lindsay with her conference coordinator, Maryann Brownlee

The speakers are prayerfully selected

Becky Fender

Iverna Tompkins

There's always time for personal ministry

The music and drama are fabulous

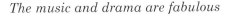

Joyce Meyer

The workshop speakers are carefully chosen, too

Dave & Jan Brunk

The David Brunk family

Somehow, I always knew that if I got "too close to God," He'd make me go to Bible school and become a missionary! So I kept my distance. As a professional student, everything was going just great. I had a mid-engine Porsche, lots of girlfriends, and some money to spare.

My two youngest brothers made a decision to "get close to Jesus," then my parents did, and they were all doing great. It looked as though I had misjudged what it meant to be a Christian. So, I decided to try living for God. When Jan and I got married, we made a decision to read our Bibles every morning and night and to pray together. We liked the changes God was making in our lives. We discovered that doing things His way was always best. Step by step, we drew closer to Him, and one day we found ourselves in Bible school. Then ministering to kids in jail and alternative high schools, in youth groups, and so on.

"Somehow" it came to our hearts to go "somewhere" in Eastern Europe or Russia. But we felt the Lord first leading us to prepare. A part of that preparation was attending CFNI's School of Missions program. During this time we dealt with some of the most practical issues of missions, as well as focusing our vision on Minsk, Belarus. Then one day, we found ourselves in the former Soviet Union. I was right; God did make me go to Bible school and become a missionary. But I was wrong! I never knew how much I'd like it! He's the best, and so is His way!

Norman and Linda Young predated our arrival, and through their relationship with the Belarussian Children's Fund, we received our required letter of invitation. We went to work learning the language and the culture. Then the work of the institute began. First, the Lord orchestrated a team - Roger and Myrna Eilers, CFNI graduates and previous school administrators; Bob and Betty Todd, CFNI grads with years of experience in school systems; and Gene and Carol Wright, teachers and school administrators. Then God brought His special "first fruits." Within the first group of 40 students, a third were musicians - all the makings of the first praise and worship team! By the second semester, we had 100 students. A gifted children's worker and worshipper, Karen Haynes joined our team.

As the work began to grow, the restrictions on religious activities grew, too. But through it all, the scope and influence continues to grow. CFN-Belarus is now one of the largest biblical institutes in the country, is among the largest humanitarian organizations, is a center for the development of contemporary praise and worship and children's ministries, and more.

Our building - a former kindergarten purchased in 1997 through a public auction - will be ready for dedication in June 1998. CFN-Belarus was the first foreign organization ever allowed to participate in an auction in Minsk! In recording all the good things God has done, I could never neglect to mention the principle that led us here: "If you want to be with Me, go where I am working!" We did, and He is!

The facility purchased in Minsk (front building)

CFN Music
Music with a message is music with a mission.

Kevin Jonas

Keith Hulen

Vision, followed by implementation, depicts the history of CFNI. Each step of progress may be traced back to a vision —that became an idea — that became a prayerful consideration — that became a reality. One area in which CFNI has moved very cautiously is the marketing of music which the Holy Spirit has given through our students and faculty in times of worship or prayer. Contrasted to a simpler life, when a shepherd boy's psalms, harped and sung while flocks grazed on the hillside could become the songbook printed in every Holy Bible ever to be published, our work is much more complex.

In 1994, necessity, brought on by new technology and legalities, plus a pure desire to make our anointed songs more accessible, inspired the birthing of a system titled CFN Music. Kevin Jonas, a talented by-product of CFNI, put the plan together and got it off to a good start, ably assisted by Becky Zint, Roger Hodges and Aaron Horton. After Kevin accepted a pastorate in New Jersey in 1997, Keith Hulen agreed to return as Worship leader and director of CFN Music, continuing to expand its functions. The experience Kim Moore brings from her position with a national Christian bookstore chain is invaluable in expanding the distribution base of CFN Music worldwide. Mary Beth Miller and Carla Beachy courteously assist callers to the 1-800-GOD-SONG number, answering requests for the new complete catalog, and filling orders for the variety of companion products now offered.

Beginning in the early '70s, with the first of a continuing series of yearly live worship tapes, CFN has become recognized as a forerunner in the production of worship music. With a worldwide circulation, these tapes have become a vital lifeline to the body of Christ. We are thankful for our heritage in historic and contemporary worship, but even more, we are excited about our future. New avenues of distribution and translation into other languages are now opening global opportunities. Assistance to local church music ministry is provided through not only the worship tapes and CDs, but inspiring videos, lead sheets, instrumental orchestrations, performance songbooks, lyrics for overhead projectors, tracks and more. Those desiring more information or to order products, can contact CFN Music by calling 1-800-GOD-SONG or e-mailing cfnmusic-juno.com.

In 1994, on her 80th birthday, Freda Lindsay resigned as CFN's chairman of the board. The board voted her son, Dennis Lindsay, to step into the position she was vacating, adding to it president and CEO. Freda remains actively involved in the ministry and plans to serve the Lord until He calls her to heaven. The ministry continues to move ahead and expand its vision under President Lindsay's leadership.

My Tribute

One early spring Canadian morn
A special little girl was born.
In a prairie farmhouse made of sod
Was fashioned a vessel of honor for God.
Nine years before on that same date
An awful tremor shook the Golden Gate.
From the bowels of the earth rose violent disruption
Spawning fires and death and great destruction!
I ponder – did God have a plan to touch the earth
    on April 18th – with a blast? – with a birth?
Could Mother Schimpf guess as she reached to take her
That this gentle babe would become an earth-shaker?
…Who would hear God's call and obey HIS voice.
Be joined to the man of HIS own choice
…Who would never give up or give in to frustrations
Till they'd spread the Gospel of Christ to the nations!
Now eight decades have come and gone
Since that eventful April dawn.
We've watched her stand steadfast in grief
Without a trace of unbelief.

We've seen her stand alone for years
Yet on her face no senseless fears;
We've watched her stand under heavy stress
Yet giving no place for bitterness.
We've seen in eyes of heaven blue
Compassion and love… and FIRMNESS, too;
For though my tribute is waxing lofty,
Hear this: The lady is no softie!
See her march with the troops like a tough foot-soldier
Off to undertake something else God told her!
Teaching, touching innumerable lives,
Extending hands through which God provides.
"YEA, MOM!" – as eternal rewards are given out
A host of her offspring will cheer and shout.
For as April's earthquake spread great devastation,
So April's earth-shaker spread so great salvation!
And this is not the end of the story;
The song goes on… "TO GOD BE THE GLORY!"

— Anna Jeanne Price

Freda is a woman of prayer, the Word and action!

President Dennis Lindsay is following his mom, leading CFN into the new millennium.

Freda's 80th birthday was celebrated in a variety of ways.

Christ For The Nations
Annual International Worship Conference

C FN's first annual Worship Conference was held in 1995. It was a success the very first year, and continues to grow. The conference is coordinated and hosted by the chair of the music department, Arlene Friesen.

Marcos Witt in concert

Arlene Friesen, Chair of CFNI's Music Department

Participants — seekers of God

Powerful praise and worship

Kent Henry in concert

Practical workshops

Christ For The Nations Institute in Belo Horizonte, Brazil

Christ For Moldova

A Courts of Praise apartment – before the renovation

After the renovation – like brand new

Now they're the most lovely apartments on campus

I n 1995, Christ For The Nations experienced the greatest financial miracle in its history. The Department of Housing and Urban Development (HUD) offered to sell CFN nine complexes containing 152 one-, two- and three-bedroom apartments for the unbelievably low price of $10. The north end of the property touched our existing campus, making the apartments a tremendous asset, especially since there always seems to be a need for more housing. The property was beautifully landscaped, with many trees. It was too great an opportunity to pass up. So President Dennis Lindsay had a penny march for the students to pay the $10.

The only problem was that several gangs had inhabited the apartments, and most needed to be completely gutted and restored. It was a long and expensive project, but June 1998 brought it to conclusion. The Courts of Praise, as the apartments were named, are like brand new, and sit on the loveliest spot on the CFNI campus.

In Belo Horizonte, a city of four million, CFNI-Brazil was started in 1995. The director is CFNI-Dallas alumnus and son of missionaries to Brazil, Gary Haynes. Over 100 students enrolled for the very first semester.

The next year, Christ for Moldova was founded — a joint ministry of CFNI and the Pentecostal Union of the Republic of Moldova. The school is located in the capital, Chisinau. The Lord moved in a miraculous way to provide a large building. Two of the staff members are CFNI-Dallas alumni.

Christ For The Nations' Executive Team

Dennis Lindsay
Chairman of the Board,
President & CEO

Randy Bozarth
Vice President &
Executive Director of
External Ministries

Larry Hill
Executive Director
of the Institute

Mark Ott
Director of
Business Affairs

Dr. Harold Reents
Academic Dean and
Director of Alumni

Eric Belcher
Director of Alumni
Ministers' Fellowship &
Int'l. Student Dean

The Dedicated Staff of
Christ For The Nations

(Due to varied responsibilities, some staff members are not pictured.)

The Institute

ONE DAY IN THE SPRING OF 1970, having been in prayer, Gordon said to Freda, "We should start a Bible School." Freda and all three of the children were reluctant, but Gordon's vision won out. That very fall, the interdenominational Bible training institute was inaugurated.

The institute was unique from its very inception. It is a place where students can drink deeply of the Word and of the Spirit.

* The daily 11 a.m. sessions are taught by prominent guest speakers, which offers the students the opportunity to hear from servants of God involved in various facets of ministry.

* The institute's powerful praise and worship is not only experienced by the students, but by millions of others through cassette tape, CD and video.

* The scholarships offered to internationals who qualify are a double blessing — to the students who receive them and to the American students who have the opportunity to study with believers from around the world.

* In 1974, Dennis Lindsay took the first outreach — to Mexico; today CFNI has about a dozen faculty-led outreaches every summer.

* CFNI caters not only to young singles, but to couples, families and even retired folks. Right on the 75-acre campus, there is family housing, nursery care and an ACE school (K-12).

* There are specialized training programs available for youth, pastoral, missions and music ministries.

CFNI is a place for believers who desire to be schooled in the Word and empowered by the Spirit for Christian life and ministry!

Anointed Instructors

Vibrant Praise and Worship

Larry Hill
Executive Director of
the Institute

Physical Activities

Internationals comprise 15-20% of the student body

Large international
student body

A Life-Changing Experience

Larry and Joy Hill and family

I came to Christ For The Nations Institute in 1972 at the age of 19. At that time I had completed two years of college and knew that the Lord had a call upon my life. CFNI was the vehicle that He used to clarify and prepare me for that calling.

Since my graduation, I have spent six years as a missionary in Mexico City, five years as missions pastor in a local church, and ten wonderful years at CFNI – as a teacher, missions director, and now as the executive director of the Institute.

After five years in the ministry, I met and married my wife, Joy, who graduated from CFNI in 1979. While a student, Joy was part of Living Praise as well as the Student Council. She continued her studies at Oral Roberts University, obtaining a degree in Music, and singing with the World Action Singers. We have been blessed with three wonderful daughters, Lauren, Amber and Kristin.

During the past 22 years, I've been privileged to travel to more than 25 nations as well as to churches all over America as a missions conference speaker. We thank God for Christ For The Nations, and it is a joy to serve and continue the vision of the Lindsay family.

Rev. Larry Hill
Executive Director of Christ For The Nations Institute

Faculty of Yesteryear

John Garlock
1973 - 1994

Jim Hodges
1974 - 1986

Carroll Thompson
1972 - 1997

Pauline Parham
1971 - 1984

The Faculty of Yesteryear

Ron Wahlrobe (dec'd)
1976 - 1980

Randy Delp
1983 - 1997

Dan and Esther Marocco
1980 - 1983

Gary Osborn
1988 - 1995

The Institute Faculty – Spring 1998

THE INSTITUTE FACULTY *(alphabetically):* Eric Belcher, Walter Bietila, Randy Bozarth, John Collins, Robert Conn, Arlene Friesen, Maureen Fryer, Alta Hatcher, Jack Hatcher, Larry Hill, Sharon Hobbs, Henry Holland, Keith Hulen, Randy Jones, Leon Jordaan, Dennis Lindsay, Connie McKenzie, Mike McMenomy, Mark Ott, Dr. Harold Reents, Dr. Jeffrey Seif, Annette Smith, Dr. Duane Weis, T. Scott Wood

The Sounds of Worship
— Past & Present

Anointed praise and worship have been a trademark of this ministry. In the '50s, the big tents reverberated with the joyful sound of hundreds, often thousands, of voices, and twice as many hands, clapping to the pulsating rhythm of the Hammond organ as the tent flaps danced in the night wind. And a few saints usually made a futile attempt to dance in the sawdust!

Those were the times when the main source of Christian music was the week-day radio quartets, Charles E. Fuller and the Sunday afternoon "Old-fashioned Revival Hour," hymnal-holding church choirs, and monthly "singing conventions" where publishers pushed their latest shaped-note songbooks. Very few records were available.

At CFNI, each school day begins with prayer, songs, and often, jubilant dancing before the Lord. As students and faculty turn their eyes upon Jesus and come into his presence with thanksgiving and praise, they are changed. The inner man is strengthened, and the daily worship habit is etched into their lives, preparing them for the future ahead.

The songs they sing direct more adoration toward a faithful, loving Lord than those of earlier times, many of which were written

about the human experience, expressing anticipation of leaving this world and crossing over to a better place. No doubt there were worshippers writing songs and choruses of exaltation. But it was when cassette recorders came out, offering the opportunity for quick circulation, that a flood of new, worshipful songs burst upon the church scene.

The '70s brought not only cassette recorders, but the "Jesus People"... and right on time, CFNI! The rest is history. Students "high" on Jesus and experiencing a new awareness of a holy God, brought forth inspired new songs of the Spirit, some so anointed they were destined to spark renewal for many years to come. (See page 119.) Today it is not uncommon to hear on the radio or TV varying arrangements of "Mighty Warrior" (Graafsma), "Ah Lord God" (Chance), "As the Deer" (Nystrom), "I Worship You, Almighty God" (Corbett), and others written by our students and alumni.

How far we've come! Fresh songs of praise fill homes across the land as DAYSTAR Television Network sends out our new program. A touch of a digital button and Kevin Jonas fills the car with "The power and the glory of His Name," and Aaron Horton's sweet voice bids us to "Come and seek the Lord while He may be found." What a day to be alive! The clever inventions of man carry thanks back to his Maker. (The popular Jewish singer, Streisand, was so moved by hearing "We are standing on holy ground," she put it on her latest CD for her world to hear.) The earth is the Lord's and the fulness thereof and it is our desire to load His airwaves with the sights and sounds of glorious praise, hastening the hour when the whole earth will be filled with His glory!

— *Anna Jeanne Price*

Worship – A Matter of the Heart

Jack Moore

Roger Hodges

It was as I listened to my daddy softly singing and strumming his mandolin, at home, that I decided to follow Jesus. "How can I help but love Him when He loved me so?" were the words that gripped my young heart. See, *it doesn't take a crowd to worship —* or to get saved.

"I love the way you people all sing, and how you hold up your arms to God. I'm going back to First Baptist Church and tell my people about you," Dr. W.A. Criswell commented before preaching a great message at our 1995 graduation.

(Note: A new freedom in worship is evident in many mainline churches. Music Ministers are blending fresh choruses with their hymns, and encouraging response such as clapping and raising hands. Worship seminars and the many available recordings of uninterrupted praise music, of which CFNI was a pioneer, have inspired this mainstream movement.)

W.A. Criswell

The first time I heard "How Great Thou Art," time and eternity seemed to merge. My husband-to-be, Don Price, brought it from singers in a youth camp he conducted in Sweden (1951). They had heard it from persecuted Christians in Russia, and we recorded one of the first English versions, Don soloing. Billy Graham and George Beverly Shea took the song to the world soon afterward, and it is now a favorite worship hymn, with four beautiful verses that make it a sacred masterpiece, qualified to be sung in heaven. None could sing it better than Dan Marocco, pictured at far left with four other Voice of Healing ministers, Tommy Reid, Carmine DiBiase, Don Price and Al Reid, in a '60s Missions Convention. Missions was their mission, and each one was faithful to his holy calling.

Phillips, Craig & Dean

Bill & Emogene Kaiser

Dean Romanelli

Following the Leader(s)

Worship leaders Bill and Emogene Kaiser and the devout group of early students and teachers laid a solid foundation in Biblical worship, for us to build upon. Multi-talented Dean Romanelli added much to the music scene in the '70s, setting up the Music Department and organizing / directing Living Praise, followed by Bob Mason in 1978. (*see page 91*)

Memorable Moments:

Joy Hill

Anointed Joy Hill sings "I'd Rather Have Jesus... than silver or gold... worldwide fame... men's applause... or ANYTHING," dedicated to a changed, humbled Jim Bakker just before he delivers a powerful message at Campus Church.

A visitor at graduation '98 promises to sponsor the renovation of the last remaining unit of Courts of Praise apartments. Mrs. Lindsay, 84, keeps her promise to dance a happy jig! An overjoyed African student runs to the stage to partner with her while the full-house audience applauds!

The popular group, "Phillips, Craig & Dean," three innovative Pentecostal preachers, show up at morning Chapel and lead praise and worship, for which we probably can credit Roger Hodges, one of our own innovative leaders who writes great songs and adds pizzazz to taping sessions and YFN!

Bless the photographer responsible for this! Surrounding their "Mom," are CFNI's Worship Leaders David Butterbaugh, Bryan Peterson, Kevin Jonas, Keith Hulen, and Mike Massa. All are alumni and hold pastoral positions. In January '97, Keith returned to fill the Worship Leader position and direct CFN Music operations.

We would like so much to be able to mention all the numerous leaders, instructors, and students who have been a part of us in music ministry. We know, and God knows, how important in CFN's history are the ones anointed to provide music. May He bless each one accordingly.

Utilizing Every Media

This ministry was birthed utilizing the primary media of the day — print media. The *Voice of Healing* magazine proclaimed the glorious signs and wonders taking place in crusades around the world. Christ For The Nations' Editorial Department continues to publish a dynamic, Spirit-filled magazine every month.

But by the '60s, the Church was beginning to utilize other media as well. First came radio, then films. CFN produced films like Israel on the March, Building the Walls, and Multiplying the Vision.

In the late '70s and early '80s, television became prominent, and CFN's broadcast media ministry was born. Originally, the audio/video ministry was headed by Paul Grier. Messages were duplicated on cassette tapes and videos, and sent around the world. Others followed this pioneer — Gene Steiner, Tim Malone, Lisa Thompson; presently, Christopher Holt directs the Media Department. In recent years, one of the department's most exciting projects has been the videotaping of the annual praise and worship tape, for these videos have gone all over the globe, even into countries closed to the Gospel such as Pakistan, Iran, and Bosnia.

Over the last 18 years, CFN has produced several television programs that have been viewed worldwide: Christ For the Nations

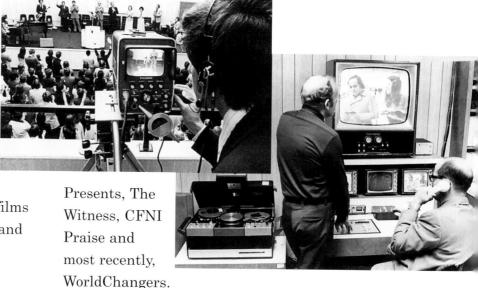

Presents, The Witness, CFNI Praise and most recently, WorldChangers.

CFNI's Media Department is training students from the U.S. and many other nations in media ministry. On a daily basis, students have an opportunity to operate cameras, mix sound, control the lighting system, and orchestrate the video recording during praise and worship and teaching sessions. Having received this training, graduates find that ministry positions are available in various parts of the world.

Carrying on the tradition of the founders to utilize every media possible to communicate the Gospel, the Media Department is reaching this sight and sound generation through contemporary communication media.

Audio engineer,
Terry McCarthy,
mixes house sound

Lighting console

Non-linear editing system

Videotape duplicator

Character generator

Video camera

Christopher Holt
confers with
WorldChangers host

Guest Speakers Through the Years

Kenneth Hagin

Marilyn Hickey

Tony Evans

Mark Buntain

Ron Luce

Dave Roever

Rob Carman

Marlin Maddoux

Barbara Wentroble

Ralph Mahoney

Mike Hayes

David Wilkerson

John Stocker

Dr. Ed Cole

Myles Munroe

Iverna Tompkins

Tommy Barnett

Dr. Jack Hayford

Winkie Pratney

Jay Sekulow

Jesse Duplantis

Richard Exley

Fred Markert

Joy Dawson

Nevers Mumba

John Osteen

Scott Hinkle

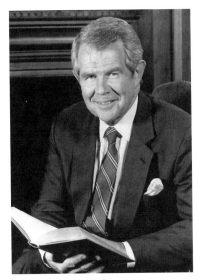

Pat Robertson

Guest Speakers Through the Years

T.L. Osborn

Michael Cavanaugh

Ben Kinchlow

James Robison

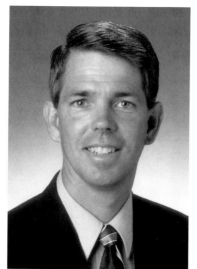

David Barton

Benny Hinn

Reinhard Bonnke

Christ For The Nations Encourages A Love for Israel

A vital part of Christ For The Nations Institute's ministry is involvement with Israel and the Jewish people. For years, CFNI has maintained a ministry center in Israel called the Jerusalem Center.

BLESS ISRAEL DAY

To keep the students informed concerning God's plan and purpose for Israel, every year in November, one day is set aside as "Bless Israel Day." The program and activities that day are centered around Israel's past, present and future — including how prophecy concerning Israel is being fulfilled in these last days and how the Church of today should relate to Israel. The evening service is the climax of the day — a celebration featuring tambourine players and dancers, drama, Hebrew songs, banners, and the blowing of the shofar.

ISRAEL OUTREACH

Another annual event is the summer outreach to Israel, which is led by Dr. Duane Weis, CFNI's chaplain and a member of the faculty, and his wife, Carolyn. Dr. Weis has a bachelor's degree

Street Rally in Tel Aviv

from the University of Houston and Southwestern Assemblies of God College, a master of science from the University of Arkansas, and a doctorate from the California Graduate School of Theology. Before coming to CFNI in 1984, he served as a pastor for 25 years. He has also been a teacher, a counselor

Coffee house ministry

and a public school administrator. The Israel outreach team goes as "ambassadors of peace"; their theme is Psalm 122:6 — "Pray for the peace of Jerusalem: May they prosper who love you."

Drama team — Jerusalem   *Children's ministry team*

The 60-75 team members minister in churches, hotels and schools; they also hold rallies on the streets of Tiberias, Haifa, and Bethlehem. In downtown Jerusalem and Tel Aviv, the huge street rallies are held in conjunction with Avi Mizrachi, a CFNI graduate who pastors a church in Tel Aviv and directs a coffee house ministry. The teams minister through drama, puppetry, tambourine, Israeli dance, and praise and worship. On the Sabbaths they spend in Israel, the team ministers at the Narkiss Street Church, which is pastored by Charles and Elizabeth Kopp, who also oversee CFN's Jerusalem Center. While in Israel, the team travels all over the land, studying the culture, language, traditions, people, religion, archaeology, and its history from biblical times to the present.

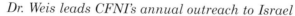

Dr. Weis leads CFNI's annual outreach to Israel

Dr. Jeffrey Seif

Jacob, Jeffrey, Patricia, Zachary

A Jew Who Found the Messiah Chairs CFNI's Jewish Studies Department

For nearly a decade, CFNI has offered a minor in Jewish Studies. Dr. Jeffrey Seif, chair of the Jewish Studies and Language departments and faculty member, is of German-Jewish extract. His mother was smuggled out of Nazi Germany during World War II; his father's family came to America from Western Europe just prior to that war. Jeff was raised in a Conservative Jewish home, attended an Orthodox Jewish synagogue, and was educated in a Jewish school.

In the wake of his acceptance of Jesus as his Messiah, Jeff responded to the call to ministry and furthered his education through Moody Bible Institute, Southern Methodist University's Perkins School of Theology, Trinity Seminary and the Graduate Theological Foundation. He was initially ordained as a Southern Baptist, worked with Zola Levitt on Christian television, and was a missionary with the American Board of Missions to the Jews. Jeff received the baptism in the Holy Spirit at CFNI, and has been on the staff for nine years. Dr. Seif has authored several books and presently pastors DeSoto Community Church in addition to serving at CFNI. He and his wife, Patricia — an accomplished counselor with a Texas school district — have two boys, Jacob (9) and Zachary (6).

Music and the Arts

Arlene Friesen and Anna Jeanne Price

Directed by Dean Romanelli from 1974-78, the first LP — a powerful, cutting-edge troupe

CFNI's Music Department has been built upon the scriptural understanding that the highest purpose of music and related arts is to minister unto the Lord — as the Levite priests did in the time of David. At CFNI, not only music, but the movement and visual arts are given creative expression in worship and as a method of evangelism.

LIVING PRAISE (LP)

Like an unbroken thread, the musical group known as Living Praise has continued to represent the vision and the dynamic musical expression of CFNI since 1974. Founded by Dean Romanelli, the first director of the institute's Music Department, and his wife Jeanne, Living Praise has carried the anointing to bring people into God's presence all over North America and to many other nations. A powerful training ground for CFNI music students, the rosters of participants over the past two dozen years read like a "Who's Who" of future pastors and worship and ministry leaders.

A 1980 appearance on 100 Huntley Street in Toronto, Canada, with Bob and Debbie Mason, the LP directors with longest tenure as directors so far — 1978-85

Al and Judy Keech (1988-89) at piano — the last directors with the combined responsibility of directing LP and the entire Music Department

Bill and Marilyn Hysell (center), directors of LP and the Music Department 1985-88 (A former Vegas show drummer and band leader, Bill met Marilyn when both were CFNI students in LP. He is now a pastor in Dallas.)

During the time Keith Hulen (front right, with Kerri) led LP (1989-92), his duties rapidly increased: he acquired a wife (Kerri, whom he met at CFNI) and became CFNI's worship leader. Today Keith is director of CFN Music. For some time, he was capably assisted by singer-composer Shannon (Fogal) Wexelberg (behind Keith)

Dean (front row, holding trombone) and Patty Demos took the baton from Kevin and Denise Jonas, serving LP (1993-95) while two of their children attended CFNI

Randy (back row, second from left) and Cheri Cochran (kneeling at left), another talented pair who met as students, directed LP 1995-97

LP's current directors – Shawn and Sandy (Grant) Nemeth (center) – are alumni. Though downsized for simpler logistics, the group presently includes internationals from Russia, Siberia, Bulgaria, Poland, Mexico and England.

A music ministry with an emphasis on signs and wonders, the Luminaires were a full-time traveling (by faith) ensemble of former CFNI students directed by John and Dean Guest. For three years, the group ministered around the world.

David's Key – another alumni music group under the leadership of Steve and Robin Bowersox, later joined by Robin's gifted and anointed mother, Nancy Fenstermacher (third from right)

From 1975 to 1992, Signs of Love (SOL) was a dynamic music ministry outreach with enormous appeal to both the hearing and the deaf.

Founded by Terry and Becky Thompson, its praise and worship and special music was accompanied by sign language and powerful skits reaching the lost and the broken-hearted.

1990 SOL with directors Michael and Casey Ball (center back)

Kevin and Denise Jonas (center), directors of SOL 1990-92, also directed the merged SOL/LP team the following year. That same year, Kevin became CFNI's worship leader and pioneered CFN's recording /publishing division known as CFN Music

Others who have led in areas of deaf ministry include: Louise Willard Derrick, Alan Gray, Alan Christiani, Jeanette Carver Harrell, Debbie Stewart Tzolov, Emilie Baumgartner Carothers

Pete and Dottie Bailey – SOL 1983-85

Mike and Sharon Teninty – SOL directors 1985-89, a very productive era for this unique song and drama group

A 1992 College Days presentation featuring LP and SOL. The colorful praise banners were designed and created by Quinett Sherrer during classes she conducted while a student. Arts other than music– banners, pageantry, drama and dance – are included in the variety of expressions from which CFNI students draw in their ministry to and for the Lord.

Excellent flutist Ela Brandys (LP '98) and her sister Eva, daughters of a Polish pastor, both received full music scholarships from a nearby four-year college.

Artistic and exuberant movement is often included in morning chapel and services at CFNI as a creative expression in praise and worship. (Praisers with tambourines are currently led by Brandi Nabors.)

Malaysian student Magrate Yap (right) developed the art of patterned tambourine choreography structured into a series of classes now offered through the Music Department.

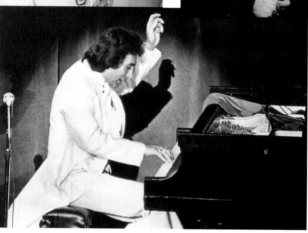

With his background as a member of one of the world's most famous opera companies, Kammersaenger Reid Bunger made an unforgettable impression on voice students during his four years as instructor and concert choir director. George Shaw (pictured with Reid) and other future worship leaders received valuable coaching.

A memorable benefit concert by Dino Kartsonakis initiated a new Baldwin concert grand piano into musical service at CFNI. Cheryl McSpadden Kartsonakis was a CFNI student and LP vocalist prior to her marriage to the talented artist.

An evening of testimony and worship during the 1995 Worship Conference included a rare duet by Dennis Jernigan and Matthew Ward, both of whom wield a wholesome influence in contemporary music.

In his native Chile, Humberto Valenzuela sang the leading role in "Jesus Christ SuperStar." A dancer in the show invited him to church, where the One who was only the character he had portrayed became his Savior. He came to CFNI to learn of Jesus and use his beautiful voice to glorify Him, which he accomplished unforgettably in our 1992 version of "Testimony Time in Heaven."

In the beautiful video of Light to the Nations, worshipful moments from the 1997 Worship Conference, a team of young worshippers led by Patti Friesen expressed their prayer through dance.

"Creative Musical Drama," *a workshop for the development of artistic expression in all aspects of drama presentation, as well as mime and dance, teaches students how to capture special moments in time and drive them into the hearts of others. Founded by Anna Jeanne Price and Rayanna Fields in 1988, this creative ministry outlet has become an indispensable feature of the music/arts department. In addition to acquired skills, Mrs. Fields has a special anointing for writing and producing.*

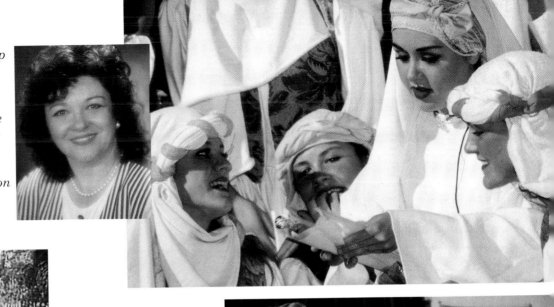

The CFNI Orchestra has enhanced worship and special musical events through expert leadership of directors such as Dr. Richard Lamb, Art Osborne, Mike Luckett, Alex Cauthen and Mark Black.

A companion product to our annual worship tape, the "Spirit Come" video provides an artful blend of voices, instruments and scenery to offer Christian television stations. It is featured on CFNI's new weekly telecast on Daystar Network.

Violinist Darek Dowgielewicz, our first student from Poland, shares the stage with Anna Jeanne Price in a musical highlight of artistic excellence and inspiration. Associated with the Lindsays since the "Voice of Healing" days, Anna Jeanne has through the years contributed the wealth of her experience in ministry, missions and music as a beloved advisor to the music/arts department.

This scene from the third annual CFN Worship Conference features the CFN Praise Band, the Chapel Choir, and tambourinists, led by worship director Keith Hulen in a chorus of praise. **"Let everything that hath breath praise the Lord"** *is an exhortation that sums up CFN's approach to musical and artistic expression.*

The Children Are Discipled, Too!

Sharon Hobbs
Christian Education Director

The Christian education director, Sharon Hobbs, oversees the programs for children from birth through grade school. Besides ministering to the children, Sharon and her assistant, Connie McKenzie, train CFNI students to do the same.

In 1990, CFNI added an on-campus Accelerated Christian Education (A.C.E.) school — Christ For The Nations Academy — for children of students and staff. The goal of the CFNA staff is to train the youth under their care — grades 1-12 — academically as well as help them develop spiritually.

Connie McKenzie
Assistant Christian Education Director

From the earliest years, families have been a priority at CFNI. While dads and moms are being trained, the children are being discipled in the ways of God, too. Even the little toddlers are not only taught the Word, but to enter wholeheartedly into praise and worship.

CFNI students desiring to learn to minister to children assist in every facet — nursery, children's church, A.C.E. school, and youth ministry — through the student ministry program.

CFNI's top notch children's ministry

*Christ For The Nations Academy —
an academic and spiritual training ground*

A Passion for the Lost

Every spring, CFNI presents a missions conference with several inspiring guest speakers — for the students and anyone who would like to stoke the fires of passion for the multitudes yet unreached with the Gospel. Scott Wood, institute missions director, presently hosts the conference.

T. Scott Wood

Bill Stearns

Fred Markert

Jim Goll

A Heart for the World

I n 1974, Dennis Lindsay led CFNI's first outreach. The team travelled past the borders of Texas, down into Mexico, to share the love of Jesus. Today, CFNI's summer outreach teams spread across the world to approximately a dozen locations.

Jamaica

South America

Russia

Evangelism —
The Key to Taking Christ to the Nations

*Randy Jones
Director of Evangelism*

CFNI not only teaches evangelism, but gives students lots of opportunities to gain practical experience.

CFNI goes beyond just teaching evangelism in the classroom. Every CFNI student is required to participate in a student ministry each semester, and most of them are evangelistic in nature. The opportunities offered are diverse — from the streets of the metroplex to the nursing homes.

Christ For The Nations Institute's
School of Missions

The School of Missions (SM) is a two-faceted program for equipping men and women to minister in cultural settings different from their own. In one intensive semester, students are immersed in classroom training specifically designed for those called to missions, including how to adapt to a foreign culture. The second facet is a one-year internship on the field with a seasoned missionary.

T. Scott Wood
Director of
School of Missions

Internship with seasoned missionaries

Practical classroom teaching

Christ For The Nations Institute's School of Youth Ministry

Serious training

The School of Youth Ministry is a unique training program especially for those who feel called to impact the lives of teenagers in the local church, in the community, and in other nations.

The program provides a course of study and practical training that is both theologically sound and relevant to today's complex youth culture. The classes are taught by instructors who have been successful in youth ministry. Participants in the program have an opportunity to work with a metroplex youth group to put their training into practice.

*John Collins
Director of Youth
Ministries*

*Mike McMenomey
Director of School of
Youth Ministries*

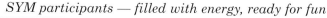

SYM participants — filled with energy, ready for fun

Christ For The Nations Institute's School of Pastoral Ministry

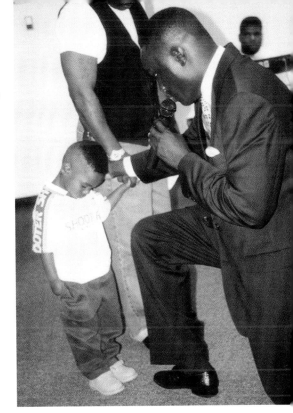

T he School of Pastoral Ministry (SPM) is an innovative program using Jesus' methods of leadership training — instruction, example, correction and participation.

Jesus wasn't interested in drawing crowds; His goal was to produce true disciples. SPM follows Jesus' example. We recognize that the challenges facing tomorrow's Church will be met through men and women being trained today for ministry. The vision of SPM is to teach students how to be effective leaders, and then give them the opportunity to put into practice what they have been taught.

Ministry in the local church

Dr. Jack Hatcher
Director of School of Pastoral Ministries

Special guest lecturer

The External Ministries

D URING CHRIST FOR THE Nations' 50 years of ministry, a variety of missions endeavors have been established — the Native Church program, the Literature Crusade, Global Assistance (relief), plus support for Israel and orphanages.

In 1993, the Christ For The Nations Association of Bible Schools was launched, and already there are 40 schools, 11 of which are in the 10-40 window. Our goal is to have 50 associated schools by the year 2000.

Randy Bozarth
CFN Vice President and
Executive Director of
External Ministries

External Ministries

Randy and Susan Bozarth

As I reflect on my life, I remember the faithful testimony of my parents, Bob and Verle Bozarth. They were married 51 years ago, and are still sweethearts today.

The impact of Gordon and Freda Lindsay's ministry on my life began many years ago. In 1949, my aunt and uncle received their first *The Voice of Healing* magazine after attending a William Branham meeting. My parents read in the magazine that a Rev. James Drush would be conducting a series of meetings in a nearby town. They attended, and on a December Friday evening in 1950, when I was only 18 months old, my parents gave their lives to the Lord. Since that night, their commitment to Christ has affected hundreds, including many family members.

I thank the Lord for my Christian upbringing. After high school, I joined the Navy. Immediately after my discharge, I met Susan. We married and started assisting in a church. In 1975, Susan and I and our two-year-old, Todd, came to Christ For The Nations Institute.

After leaving CFNI in 1977, Susan and I became involved in full-time ministry, pastoring and pioneering churches in the Southeast.

In mid '92, after establishing and pastoring a church on Hilton Head Island, South Carolina, we sensed a strong witness to move into missions. We knew the best place for that was at CFN.

I joined the staff of CFN that year as an instructor. Shortly thereafter, I was appointed the director of CFN's External Ministries and became part of President Lindsay's executive team. I also oversee the CFN archives - to preserve the organization's Pentecostal heritage.

The Bozarth Family

In 1997, I helped to found CFN's Campus Church and continue to offer leadership to its five-fold ministry team. That same year, I was given the honor of being appointed CFN's vice president.

Our two sons, Todd (25) and Chad (14) are both serving the Lord. Todd has a lovely wife, Lori, and they gave us our beautiful granddaughter, Abigail.

Susan and I are thrilled with the opportunity to serve this great world missions organization called Christ For The Nations.

— ***Randy Bozarth***

Kenya

Native Church Foundation

S ince 1961, CFN's Native Church program has helped finance building over 10,000 churches for needy congregations in Third-World countries. The congregation buys the land and starts the building, then CFN sponsors provide the funds for roofing material, windows, doors, etc. — things the people cannot afford to purchase themselves.

Mexico

Philippines

Ecuador

Literature for the Nations

Gordon Lindsay recognized the need for Christian magazines and books: "The power of the printed word is something recognized and shrewdly exploited by the evil forces of this world... The cults and isms send out a steady flow of literature calculated to influence and brainwash the people into accepting their false and deceptive philosophies. The pornographic press turns out an avalanche of the vilest and most corrupt kind of reading matter, flaunting it unashamedly on every newsstand."

That's why he started the Literature Crusade. For more than 30 years, CFN has produced Christian literature — 13 of Gordon's books and four books by other authors for children — to be sent without charge to missionaries, national pastors and lay workers. These books have been distributed in 120 developing nations, some of them in nearly 80 languages. Only God knows the far-reaching impact the over 50 million books CFN has sent have had upon the world.

Israel tour group '93

The Garden Tomb

A Heart for Israel

In October of 1967, Gordon and Freda Lindsay took their first tour group to experience the land of Israel. After Gordon's death, Freda kept up the tradition, and to date has taken 32 tour groups.

The Upper Room

The Red Sea

Orphans

Freda Lindsay holding twins in a Jamaican orphanage

Edith Greet holding one of India's castaways

Christ For the Nations helps feed and clothe orphans in India, Bethlehem, Romania, Minsk, Bulgaria and other nations.

A SACRIFICIAL LIFE

In 1947, Edith Greet left family, fiance' and friends in America and headed for India. She arrived in Kerala with a total of $12 in her pocket. After rescuing and training thousands of girls from the streets, she wrote Freda Lindsay:

"For two years, I was losing my sight. Last November, an operation was performed, and now I walk and see good. One by one, God is answering each prayer in His time. Our piggery, the chicken farm, and a few rubber, coconut and banana trees are now a reality. They help feed the hundreds of children we have in our orphanage and centers. My assistant and administrator, Thomas, is a real help with the big projects. I do keep so busy even from my wheelchair (due to my health), for I'm still the president. For these 50 years in India, I have lived every hour by His grace and power, and I feel assured that God will guide me in the right path. I know all things will pale, crumble and fall before God fails me — a precious passport for me these years. I have much for which to praise Him. Again, Freda, I want to thank you for these years of friendship."

Jesus said, "Let the children be filled first" (Mk. 7:27).
"Let the little children come to Me" (Mk. 10:14).
"He took them up in His arms, put His hands on them, and blessed them" (Mk. 10:16).
"Whoever does not receive the kingdom of God as a little child, will by no means enter it" (Mk. 10:15).

Edith's orphanage in India — Bethel

A Partnership

Taking an opportunity to do something significant for God and our fellow man, in recent years Global Assistance has joined with CFN to touch the lonely and hurting. Working together, nearly $70 million in humanitarian aid has been distributed.

Global Assistance is an organization committed to assisting those suffering from disasters throughout the world. Basic needs, such as clean water, minimum nutrition, sanitation and education are often lacking. Children usually suffer the most. Global Assistance provides care for children whose parents were killed or taken away.

Norman and Linda Young

Often they roam the streets, barefoot, looking for food. Toddlers sit passively on the floor or on their beds. As you read this, scores of orphans are being cared for in the former Soviet Union. A massive effort is under way to provide a plant that can produce baby formula and dry milk products for children.

What is the most effective means to change a nation locked in an anti-God mentality? That has been the question for evangelical churches ministering in the former Soviet Union. Our first answer, evangelization, would be a part, but not the whole. The most effective means of change is redirecting the pliable minds of children toward God. The Bible tells of the importance of training the children.

A few years ago, Global Assistance, at the encouragement of Dr. Bill Basansky, a pastor in Florida, arranged for a huge shipment of humanitarian aid to Ukraine. The gift touched the hearts of the nation's leadership and opened the door for Basansky to meet with high level government officials of Ukraine. The result? They asked him to prepare Christian curriculum for the nation's public school system which is now in use there. Changing the youth will change the nation.

It was a significant day when the executive health officials in Minsk, Belarus, received with profound gratitude an ambulance completely equipped with emergency life-saving supplies. Trained medical technicians from America assisted them in its operation. This act of kindness made it easier for these former Communist leaders to understand God's love.

— ***Norman and Linda Young***

The Youngs at Red Square

The ambulance donated

Note: Before founding Global Assistance, Norman and Linda Young served on the staff of Christ For The Nations for 14 years. During that time Linda's father, Walter Helzer, who is now gone on to his reward, volunteered his services at the CFN campus carpentry shop.

Faith World Bible College in Harare, Zimbabwe

Association of Bible Schools

CFN's Association of Bible Schools (CFNABS) was founded in 1993 to provide fellowship, networking and accountability to leaders of Spirit-filled Bible schools around the world.

Over the last 25 years, CFN's institute has produced a number of alumni who share CFNI's passion to train leaders for the work of the ministry. Many have returned to their homeland to pursue their God-given vision to start training centers, patterning them after CFNI. In addition, leaders of independent Bible training centers, knowing CFNI's excellent reputation, seek relationship through CFNABS. The association is presently represented in Africa, Europe, Eastern Europe, Asia, Central and South America, North America and the Caribbean.

CFNABS offers Bible school leaders the safety of accountability, resources, counsel and encouragement while supporting autonomy and cultural relevance. Leaders are given the means to network with other schools across the globe, mutually strengthening and supporting each other.

Belarus	*India*	*Nicaragua*
Brazil	*Israel*	*Nigeria*
Bulgaria	*Ivory Coast*	*Romania*
Canada	*Jamaica*	*South Africa*
England	*Japan*	*Uganda*
Germany	*Korea*	*Ukraine*
Ghana	*Mexico*	*Zambia*
Haiti	*Moldova*	*Zimbabwe*
Honduras	*Nepal*	*U.S.A.*

Burning Bush Bible Institute

Christ For The Nations-United Kingdom

Ivory Coast

As students at Christ For The Nations Institute-Dallas, Jason Benedict (an American) and Adebayo Ademeji (originally from Nigeria) sensed the Lord bringing them together for a specific purpose. Following graduation, Adebayo went directly to the Ivory Coast, where he started a Bible school. It was tough going alone. When Jason and his wife, Kim, joined him there in 1994, the team worked hard to revitalize the school. They have tasted the success of seeing the first graduating class of 15 receive their diplomas in October 1996. These students, having completed the two-year program, are all in the ministry today.

Working with a staff from several different nations, Jason and Kim now serve as directors of the school. With the Ivory Coast on the "sill" of the 10/40 Window, the role of this Bible School to train leaders is vitally important.

Jason and Kimberly Benedict

England

Kevin Swadling had many occasions to get acquainted with CFNI and worked at the Caribbean CFNI in Jamaica for three years. His daughters graduated from CFNI-Dallas and CFNI-Canada.

Back in England, in December 1993, he received a clear directive from the Lord to start a Bible school. Kevin's relationship with and respect for the CFNI in Dallas, Canada and Jamaica made him choose this ministry to work with from the start. He loves CFN's passion, its international vision and its spirit of excellence.

A board of trustees was formed in 1994, and by January 1995, they obtained a suitable building. Christ For The Nations-United Kingdom first opened its doors for students in September 1995. It has been growing ever since and has an important place — training leaders and hosting short-term conferences for the Church in Britain.

Kevin and Pam Swadling

Christ For The Nations Bible College-Nagaland

Faith World Bible College

Nagaland, India

Vitokhu Vito graduated from Christ For The Nations in 1978 and returned to his home in Nagaland, northeast India. In 1980, he started the Christ For The Nations Bible College in the city of Kohima, offering a four-year Bachelor of Theology program. Several hundred students have graduated from the degree program, but the number of students completing a short term of training is more than 3,000.

Before he passed away at age 59 in 1993,

Mrs. Alila Vito

Vitokhu and his students planted approximately 500 churches in Nagaland, as well as in Nepal, Bhutan and Myanmar (Burma). After his death, his widow, Alila, took up the mantle, serving as director over this school as well as a sister school in Dimapur, India.

The school emphasizes prayer, evangelism and moving in the gifts of the Holy Spirit. Many of its students come from the churches that were previously planted, and they return home after graduating to plant more.

Zimbabwe

Graduating from CFNI in 1984, Bartholomew and Appiah Manjoro worked faithfully under another graduate of CFNI in Zimbabwe in 1993. Led of the Lord, the couple started a lunch-hour prayer meeting and a counseling ministry. Soon those attending asked for fellowship times, and Faith World Ministries was born.

Building on the success of their ministry and their appreciation of the spirit of Christ For The Nations, the Manjoro's opened Faith World Bible College in January 1998. The growth of their work necessitated the purchase of property that will be home to all aspects of the ministry, where students will receive hands-on training under the capable leadership of Bartholomew and Apphia Manjoro, proud alumni of CFNI-Dallas.

Dr. Bartholomew and Appiah Manjoro and family

Doulos Bible Institute

Frank Banda (lower left) and Cristo Para Las Naciones-Mexico

India

A 1973 graduate of Christ For The Nations, Joseph Skinner planted Doulos Bible Institute in 1978, offering programs varying between one and four years of formal study. More than 500 graduates have passed through the school.

With a profound love for the spirit of Christ For The Nations in his heart, Joseph patterned Doulos Bible Institute after CFNI, emphasizing the work of the Holy Spirit in the lives of students. Combining classroom training with practical experience in church planting and missions serves to prepare the students for the ministry.

Joseph and Annie Skinner

Mexico

Amistad Christiana, a strong and growing church in Mexico City, started a Bible school in 1983 to train its leaders. As the church grew and developed a fellowship of churches with other congregations in Mexico, the need for training leaders for the nation and beyond increased. More than 1,000 students have graduated from the Bible school.

Building on the spiritual kinship between Amistad Christiana and Christ For The Nations, the leadership of the school sought strong ties with CFN's Association of Bible Schools. The lasting relationship between leaders of both bodies was confirmed when CFN granted the Bible school permission to use the Spanish name for Christ For The Nations-Mexico. It has grown into an institute renowned for excellence.

Cristo Para Las Naciones-Mexico's facility

The Fruit

WITH MORE THAN 26,000 alumni spread across the globe, some building the Kingdom via the marketplace and some through full-time ministry, Christ For The Nations Institute's influence is immeasurable. The Kingdom is expanding by leaps and bounds as alumni combine their unique, God-given abilities with the training they received at CFNI to become world changers within their spheres of influence. Already, virtually every country of the world has been touched by Christ For The Nations Institute's alumni.

Birth of a Ministry

Marty Nystrom

After graduating from ORU in 1980, I went home to Seattle and began teaching in public school. A good friend, Bonnie Laughlin, one of the partners with me in the World Action Singers, went to CFNI after ORU, and she kept telling me about the wonderful praise and worship, and urging me to enroll in summer school. Because of being featured in the TV shows, the atmosphere we were accustomed to was more of performance. Bonnie felt I needed the spiritual conditioning prevalent at CFNI. She was right, and it didn't take long for me to realize I was there by divine appointment. My two roommates and I prayed and fasted together, hungering for holiness. I began to experience worship as never before, and my spirit was nourished in the classes and services.

One afternoon, at the piano upstairs in Gordon Lindsay Hall, words began to form and fit chord progressions coming out of my head. The Psalm for that day, the 19th day of a 21-day fast (taking only water) was on my mind: "As the deer panteth after the water brooks, so panteth my soul after Thee, O God" (Psa. 42:1). My spirit agreed with the psalmist's words, and more came. I sang the song to the Lord, gave it to the worship leader the next day, and forgot about it. The worship leader, David Butterbaugh, put it on the next CFNI worship tape; later, Bob Mason used it with verses on a Living Praise tape, and it continues to stay in the "Top 25" in American churches, as well as in several countries where it has been translated. That day marked the beginning of a new identity and ministry for me.

Soon after I led worship on the Hosanna! Integrity tape "Forever Grateful," I was hired by that company as the song development manager, reviewing all the thousands of songs submitted and helping choose those to go on new projects.

Our family enjoyed three years there in Mobile, Alabama, and left Hosanna with good relations intact, to settle back in the Seattle area. My wife, Jeanne, has a degree in music therapy, and also experienced a semester at CFNI. Our boys, Nathan and Benjamin, are now 11 and 7.

I presently enjoy a part-time worship leader position at a church of 2,500 pastored by Jim Hayford, which affords me the liberty to fulfill ten engagements a year in the U.S. and overseas.

—*Marty Nystrom*

Reaching His Continent for God

Ezekiel Guti, with wife Eunor
and family

Ezekiel Guti

Ezekiel Guti came as a student to CFNI having already established 80 churches in his homeland of Zimbabwe. Dr. Guti says, *"Christ For The Nations helped me to broaden my mind."* He learned a lot from Gordon Lindsay and believes that his life and teaching had a great impact on his life. He is thankful for the motherly love he has received from Mrs. Lindsay.

He returned to Zimbabwe after graduating in 1972. His ministry, Forward in Faith Ministries expanded to more than 3,000 churches in Zimbabwe and has spread to 19 countries. The ministry consists of a diversity of ministries including child evangelism, youth, ministry to the blind, women and men's fellowships, business fellowship, chaplain's ministry, ministry to sons and daughters of pastors, and Bible school training. Their training ministry also equips in a number of practical skills, including dressmaking, cooking, carpentry, agriculture, horticulture, painting, welding, mechanics, and

adult literacy. They have established three Bible schools in Zimbabwe, one in Zambia, one in South Africa and two in Mozambique. Other areas of ministry include an orphanage center, ministry to widows and the elderly, and a newly-formed street kids ministry.

In Zimbabwe, Forward in Faith Ministries has impacted every city, town and nearly every village.

It is known as the fastest growing church in Zimbabwe, with more than 1.5 million members. The ministry continues to grow as Dr. Guti passionately organizes, plans, trains, sends and encourages pastors, evangelists and youth ministers. He encourages the women as well because he believes they are the backbone and supporters of the ministry. He has a great vision for many souls to be saved, and preaches Christ, the Chief cornerstone, building upon the foundation of the apostles and the prophets.

He ministers in the power of the Holy Spirit and enjoys much acceptance throughout Zimbabwe.

Captivated by "The Voice of Healing"

Dr. E.J.R. Belcher

My interest in Christ For The Nations sprang from two of the very first copies of *The Voice of Healing* magazines 48 years ago. My wife, Melva, and I were on vacation in our homeland of New Zealand. I became so absorbed in what God was doing in the USA, and was reading and re-reading *Voice of Healing*. My young bride reminded me that we had worked hard and paid to enjoy the beautiful New Zealand environment.

Later, however, my particular interest was to prove providential when our son was born with a crippled foot. Many of our friends were praying for Robin, whose legs were in a metal brace. He had been diagnosed as having to wear surgical boots till five years of age.

We sent a prayer request to Gordon Lindsay and William Branham. They sent a prayer cloth, which we fastened to his baby clothing. The next time we visited the specialist, imagine our rejoicing on hearing the doctor proclaim, "This leg has come around with a bang!" Robin never wore that brace again and never wore surgical corrective boots!

I have often recalled the way in which I was captivated by *The Voice of Healing* content and how I wondered if this was a personal focus for my ministry. I saw it much more clearly in perspective when I was engaged as a teacher and registrar at CFNI 26 years later.

When we left New Zealand in 1977, I had no idea that I would later be joining the faculty of CFNI. The Lord, I believe, gave me a choice as I approached 50: "You can stay in New Zealand as vice president of your denomination, and coast into a somewhat comfortable retirement. However, if you choose, with your wife and family to forsake all and go to the land I have put on your heart, I will renew your vision."

Three years after coming to the USA, I applied to CFNI. Mrs. Lindsay prayed for six months before accepting this man from "down under," who was an "unknown quantity." When my son helped me unpack my boxes of books, the first thing he took out was my two original *Voice of Healing* magazines. I had brought them back to the place where they were first published! He then took out an old transistor radio and flipped on the switch. Amazingly, Robin heard his own healing testimony at that precise moment, for we had told Mrs. Lindsay of the healing and she was speaking of it on a Christian radio program.

Eric and Melva Belcher and son, Robin

When I arrived at Christ For The Nations on a very cold December evening, I took off my shoes in front of its headquarters. I told the Lord that as a teacher and administrator I would endeavor to maintain the balanced ministry which I know all of Gordon Lindsay's life portrayed.

Now 15 years later, I have the freedom to minister throughout much of the world "thanks to *The Voice of Healing* and Christ For The Nations.

—*Dr. E.J.R. Belcher*

The Cure for Addiction

Scott Hinkle

As a 19-year-old Jewish heroin addict from New Jersey, I was locked up in a psychiatric ward and later sent out of state to live with relatives. On March 24, 1970, as the result of another former drug user speaking in a high school assembly, I gave my life to Jesus — at a root beer stand in a parking lot.

Immediately, I began to tell others what Jesus had done in my life. Soon after my conversion, I began to travel and share my testimony in churches, youth meetings, etc. The young evangelist who led me to Christ (Charles McPheeters) told me about a new Bible school that had just opened in Dallas — Christ For The Nations Institute. Because I knew God had called me to the ministry, I wanted to prepare. God miraculously provided the funds for me to enroll in August 1971. I was impacted by the reality of the Holy Spirit's power, as well as the Word of God. Beyond preparation for ministry, my life was transformed at CFNI.

It was a great privilege to sit under the ministry of Gordon Lindsay and others. The building blocks of prayer, faith, integrity, God's Word, and soul-winning were firmly laid in my life. At the end of my first year, during the peak of the Jesus Movement, I returned to Denver to launch a multifaceted street ministry called The Holy Ghost Repair Service. Fifteen months later, I returned for my summer and second year of studies.

In 1981, my wife, Nancy, and I launched our own Scott Hinkle Evangelistic Association as a vehicle to facilitate evangelistic crusades and outreaches across the U.S. Networking with like-focused ministries, including two led by other CFNI alumni, we founded the National Street Ministries Conference in 1984. The conference has helped train thousands of workers, leaders, pastors and evangelists for frontline evangelism throughout America, and now in London.

Today, based in Phoenix, Arizona, our ministry continues to grow. Thousands of gang members and inner-city youth have been impacted by the Gospel.

Nancy and I praise God for our time as students at CFNI. We have constantly drawn on the work God did in our lives in those early years, as we continue to pursue fulfilling our part in the Great Commission.

—*Scott Hinkle*

"To the Jew First..."

*Ray and Sharon Sanders,
Jerusalem, Israel*

The Sanders' headquarters in Jerusalem

As an Iowa State University grad in agri-business, and a farm real estate broker, I answered God's call to full-time service in 1983. My wife, Sharon, had spent 20 years as a legal and circuit court judge's secretary. Both of us were born again and Spirit-filled in the early '70s.

During 1983-1985, while attending Christ For The Nations Institute, Sharon became Mrs. Lindsay's secretary, while I was the campus yearbook editor.

In 1985, we went to Jerusalem, where we established Christian Friends of Israel — a ministry of reconciliation between Christians and Jews. Our distribution center has helped 125,000 primarily Russian immigrants with tons of clothing, bedding and other supplies. We often travel with and oversee an international staff of volunteers, visiting nations to find and help Holocaust survivors immigrate to Israel.

The motivation for our outreach over the past 12 years is a desire for the unconditional love of Jesus to be shown to the Jewish people. We endeavor to manifest that love as we speak to many congregations.

—*Ray Sanders*

Ministry and Business: A Dual Track

Rita and Peter Tsukahira, Daniel and Nina

The suicide of my university roommate and best friend triggered in me a painful search for truth that only ended when I asked Jesus to be the Lord of my life. Before then, I thought God was a *cosmic force* dwelling in some remote part of the universe. When my friend died, my self-confidence was gone and I saw that the idea of God as an impersonal cosmic being was a cruel hoax. The true God would be here among us, not someone distant and cold. He would be a genuine person of great compassion and wisdom, unafraid of self-sacrifice, which is the ultimate test of love. When I was confronted with the truth of Jesus, I knew He was that One.

Although Rita's family was not religious according to orthodox tradition, they lived in a world that was deeply Jewish in its roots. On Passover, after eating the *seder* meal, they would open the door for Elijah, the one who would come before the Messiah, and she would think *"Maybe this year, he is going to come."* Looking back now, she recognizes there was a longing and desire within her for the Messiah's coming. After crying out to God on *Yom Kippur*, the Day of Atonement,

Yeshua (Jesus) revealed Himself to her, and she has never doubted He is the Messiah of my people.

After coming to the Lord out of the hippie culture in New Mexico, God spoke in a clear voice that we would go to both Japan and Israel. But before "sending" us, the Lord took us to CFNI in 1974, where a world vision and the conviction of Israel's unique role in His plan were firmly planted in our hearts.

While a student, I worked in a local bank. The combination of ministry and business was to be, for a season, a dual-track calling.

Business became the "vehicle" for opening doors into the lives of the people in both countries where we would go. In Tokyo, we helped lead an international fellowship and worked with university students on the campus where Rita taught. In 1987, we came on *aliyah* (as immigrants) to Israel. Four years later, after SCUD missiles fell on our city, the Lord raised up a pioneering congregation to witness the fire of revival that will once again descend upon Mount Carmel! So today, Peter and Rita Tsukahira are citizens of Israel and pastor an indigenous congregation on Mount Carmel in Haifa.

We have seen in our own lives the fulfillment of Isaiah 41:9. He has taken us "from the ends of the earth," and "called us from its remotest parts."

—*Peter Tsukahira*

Pivotal Decisions

*Mark and Lyn Ott
and family*

Each of us make decisions that change the course of our lives. My decision to attend CFNI in 1972 was one of those pivotal decisions. I can see the evidence of God's hand in my life through CFNI.

It began in October 1972, at a Christ For The Nations conference and banquet in Oakland, California. At the banquet, my mom (Doris Ott) was seated next to another woman. Upon hearing about me, she insisted on taking mom to meet the Lindsays following the banquet to receive more information about the school. It turned out that she was Ruth Eckhart, Gordon's sister.

The Lindsays were gracious and encouraging. Gordon gave mom the last catalog they had, and commented that God wanted me at CFNI and that I would be used there. I don't think Mom expected me to go since I had other plans for college. However, I finished high school early and had a semester free. I thought it would be a good opportunity to spend some time strengthening my faith before attending college.

Also, I had met a girl from Oklahoma. And Texas was a lot closer to Oklahoma than California (so much for spiritual motives)! But God used that to get me where He wanted me. I only planned on attending CFNI for one semester. Little did I know what God had in store for me.

That first semester changed my life, my way of thinking and my perspective. As part of a student body of 120, we were challenged daily by chapel, our classes and the guest speakers. I obtained a world vision. It caused me to seek God for His purposes in my life rather than seeking His blessing on my plans.

That semester would be the last one Gordon Lindsay taught. I will always appreciate the opportunity to sit in his classes and to see how he and Mrs. Lindsay lived their lives on campus. He had no pretensions, was a humble leader with a dry sense of humor, and made it a point to meet all the students. These left an impression on me, along with his balance and character.

On April 1, 1973, we were all shocked as Gordon Lindsay was called home during a Sunday service. Although a tragic loss, it caused the students to intensify their focus on the Lord. A significant portion of that graduating class went into active ministry.

My future wife, Lyn, began classes in the fall of 1973. We married the following summer as I finished my second year at CFNI. During that year, I began working in CFN's business office. I have worked at CFNI in various capacities since then, serving in the business office as well as teaching.

The years have come and gone, and I'm still in Dallas, and still involved at CFNI, presently as director of business affairs. My time at CFNI has been richly rewarding. God has blessed my family, and together we have seen CFNI grow in its outreach, its physical structures, and in the number of lives affected. That initial decision proved to be a life changer: in my personal life, my vocation, and my family (which includes two children, both grown and married).

—Mark Ott

Foundations for Ministry

Nancy Stainback

I n the late '70s, Keith and I were part of a contemporary Christian band that worked primarily in the South. Having met Bob and Debbie Mason and Spencer and Cyndy Nordyke, we knew a little about CFNI. After Keith and I married, God began to deal with us about the direction of our lives. In 1984, while leading worship in a church in Tyler, Texas, we began to feel a leading toward attending the school. We quickly sold our home for the price offered and used the equity to attend CFNI. Our oldest son, Kris, was three years old and Seth was less than one. Their Christian education and foundation began at CFNI as well.

In the middle of our first year at CFNI, "The PTL Club" announced a nationwide talent search, and Dallas was one of the cities named. I was not really interested in becoming a part of PTL, but a dear friend of ours, Anna Jeanne Price, insisted on taking me, "Darek D.," and Bill and Marilyn Hysell to the auditions. Out of respect for her, I went along. The rest is history. Director Paul Ferrin wanted us.

Keith and I graduated in May 1986, before moving to South Carolina. I was hired by the PTL Television Network as one of the "PTL Singers" featured daily across the U.S. and other countries. Six months after I signed on, the Bakkers resigned. The next three years, the remaining members of the PTL family were privileged to minister to millions. I have never regretted the time spent there. After that ministry ended in 1990, God opened doors into unusual places of service. I have sung for presidents, movie stars, and thousands of everyday folk, traveling all over the world. Yet nothing compares to leading in the worship of Almighty God.

Keith and I have just celebrated our 18th anniversary, still traveling much in ministry. We also serve in our local church when we are home — I sing with the praise team and Keith plays drums. Our son, Kris, will graduate next year and says he wants to become a film producer. Seth, 14, is doing well on the guitar and writing music. We are so grateful for the time spent at CFNI. The training we received was invaluable.

— *Nancy Stainback*

Dedicated to India

I attended CFNI in 1976. After my first year, I went to India on the first ministry world tour conducted by CFNI. It was during this ministry tour that I received a clear vision for missions with an emphasis on India. When I returned to complete my second year at CFNI, this call was confirmed through sessions of prayer and fasting. In 1978, I returned to India and worked with Miss Edith Greet of Bethel Girls' Town, Cochin, Kerala. For three years I worked in India and Sri Lanka, mostly in children's evangelistic ministry. In 1980, I returned to the States, where I met my husband-to-be, John Sylvester, who was attending CFNI on a foreign student scholarship. John completed his one year, we married, and returned the same year to Allahabad, India, John's home. We have been laboring there for the Lord for the past 16 years. We have one daughter, Esther, who is 15 years old.

John is founder and executive director of *Stewards' Trust,* a Christian relief, rehabilitation and community development organization. Projects are being run in rural areas with integrated programs consisting of primary education, adult literacy, medical and family health programs, agricultural and water management.

I am director of administration of Stewards' Trust. I also teach in India's Bible Training Institute, an indigenous work of Sr. Rev. Sylvester, training young men for rural evangelism (majoring on the Holy Spirit and child evangelism). I conduct weekly Bible studies in my home, and I'm a lay ministry leader in the Allahabad Pentecostal Church, assisting in conducting services, delivering the Word of God, and leading worship.

John and Kay Sylvester and daughter, Esther

Maharashtra earthquake relief

John Sylvester ministering

A Family Church with a World Vision

Holly, Jonathan, Bethany and David Hummel

I attended Christ For The Nations Institute from 1974 to 1976, during which time my destiny in God was shaped. My life was especially impacted by the prayer life I developed, and the heart for missions and worship which were imparted to me while I was there. I entered CFNI as a typical 18-year-old trying to find purpose in life. But I left two years later as a man of integrity and destiny. I had a consuming passion to reach the world and take my place in the body of Christ as a servant, a worshiper and a leader

After graduation, I ministered to youth, directed youth camps — and married Holly Young in Montana. I then joined the staff at Lakewood Church in Houston, Texas, where I assisted Pastor John Osteen with the youth, bookstore, missions and music.

In 1982, I was instructed in a dream to pastor in Portland, Oregon. So my family, including 2-year-old Jonathan and 3-month-old Bethany, moved to Oregon. From the beginning, God sent faithful people to love and help in the work of Portland Victory Fellowship.

In 1991, the congregation finished construction on a beautiful building on nine acres and moved the church and Christian school there. By God's divine appointment, Freda Lindsay was visiting Portland, heard about the church and "just happened" to attend our very first service in the new facility. It was such a surprise, blessing and encouragement to have her speak a dedication over our new building. Her influence, and that of CFNI, has been a strength and part of the foundation of Portland Victory Fellowship, which was 15 years old in April, 1998.

—*David Hummel*

Portland Victory Fellowship

Worship Songs for the Japanese

Kazushi Mitani and family

I thank God for giving me the opportunity to study at CFNI. The worship service held every day at CFNI influenced me very much. I was seeking spiritual worship songs that Japanese Christians could use, and all the worship songs were wonderful. These services had an important effect upon my vision, and through them God encouraged me to start a new ministry.

After I graduated in 1983, I started a church in Kawasaki-City (next to Tokyo), as well as "Noah's Music Ministry." This ministry was to encourage Christians to worship God using songs with easy words and music because most churches in Japan were singing foreign music that had been translated. But most of the translated words didn't fit Japanese feeling because of the cultural differences. I felt a strong need to make songs for Japanese. I prayed that God would give us worship songs, and God has inspired over 350 wonderful songs. God has blessed our ministry abundantly, and most of our original songs are widely known, not only in Japan, but also in many churches overseas. We give concerts when we are requested or as the occasion arises. We also produce our original songs on CD and tape albums; we have already released 36 albums and 5 songbooks.

We have a unique system where everyone can get our tapes and CD even those people who cannot afford to buy. As I want to share God's blessing with as many people as possible, we don't have a fixed price. Some people receive the tapes free and others by giving an offering.

Another peculiarity of our ministry is that we don't mention who wrote the song, as all the songs are a precious gift from God. We just mention that all the songs belong to Noah's Music Ministry. We are also advocating the "Sharing Gospel Music" (SGM) system. We are allowing others to use our music or copy them for church use without permission and free of charge. I don't want to do this ministry for money or use it to become famous. Worship songs are a great gift from God and we should give it back to God as an offering. We must give all the glory to God.

Our church is growing and I have started on our third new building.

— **Kazushi Mitani**

Kazushi at Noah's Music Ministry studio

Reaching the Hearing Impaired

Patti Jones

In Bogota, Colombia, a city of 8 million, there are around 20,000 hearing-impaired, school-age children and young people; but it appears that less than 1,500 of them are enrolled in school. We are concerned for those who do not have the opportunity to study, and even more concerned that they learn about Jesus. As the Bible says, "How shall they hear without a preacher?" (Rom. 10:14).

In 1986, in Bogota, Colombia, with only six students, I started a school for the hearing-impaired. Today, we have 193 students, ages 3 to 20, as well as a full-time staff of 17.

From our deaf church, deaf and hearing-impaired leaders travel all over Colombia, sharing Jesus. It is our vision that every deaf person in Colombia know the good news of Jesus, and that some of them be raised up to preach and teach God's Word to other hearing-impaired people around the world.

Much of this ministry is the result of the training and anointing I received while attending Christ For The Nations Institute. I knew nothing about the hearing-impaired when I started, but through CFNI, God spoke to my heart about the deaf in Colombia, and brought me here. On the big metal map on the back wall of the CFNI platform, the light seemed to fall right on Colombia. Upon graduation, I answered God's call.

I am so grateful God led me to CFNI, because that is where my vision for the deaf began.

— ***Patti Jones***

Deaf school in Bogota, Colombia

A Construction Ministry

Terry and Bette Beatty

In the summer of '75, Bette and I were in a prayer meeting in Galesville, Wisconsin, where some CFNI graduates were sharing about how the school had changed their lives. We got so excited, we decided to visit the next week. We arrived in Dallas for the opening rally of the fall semester, and after attending classes the next day, we knew CFNI was for us!

In November, I quit my job as a masonry superintendent for a large general contractor. We had an auctioneer come and sell everything that wouldn't fit in a 4' x 6' trailer, and we and our four kids took off for Texas. The next two years were some of the best of our lives. It was great going to class and studying together. We loved our teachers and the revelation and wisdom they brought into our lives.

After graduating in May '78, we moved back to Wisconsin, where I served as an associate pastor and built houses to support the family. While out shoveling snow one night, the thought hit me: "I know a place where it doesn't do this!" That same week a letter came from CFN's business manager,

offering me the maintenance supervisor position at CFN (if I hadn't already frozen to death). After briefly considering the offer, we accepted it, and headed back to Texas as soon as school was out. Mrs. Lindsay has never forgotten our arrival. What a sight! A car full of kids and pick-up loaded with ladders, shovels, and all kinds of construction equipment, pulling the biggest U-haul we could rent!

In '85, things were not going fast enough for Mrs. L on the IB expansion, and she asked me to "go over there and get that thing moving." That began my involvement in construction at CFNI. I have overseen the Maintenance building, the Library/Chapel, an addition to the Music Building, and all the construction of the Caribbean CFNI buildings in Jamaica. The most recent project, renovation of Courts of Praise complex on the Dallas campus, is nearly completed. Our heart is in taking work-teams from here to help on mission fields.

Bette, after several years of working for CFN in various capacities — mailroom clerk, switchboard operator, and CCFNI stateside representative — is presently staying home and loving it. Last year we moved into our miracle duplex, where with 2,000 feet of space we have room for our four children, their wonderful spouses, and our almost-a-dozen grandchildren to visit us all at once! The Lord has been good to us!

—Terry Beatty

Ram Zango

From Voodoo to Jesus

I was born to an African voodoo tribal chief in French-speaking Burkina Faso. My father taught me witchcraft in great detail, sacrifices to appease the gods, black power, red and yellow power.

While attending the university, I taught math in high school. One of my students invited me to a healing crusade held by an evangelist from France. Very skeptical, I decided to go. Seated in front of me was a 17-year-old, crippled from birth. I saw this person suddenly shake, then walk, jump and praise God. I believed. I went forward to accept Jesus, "never to turn back."

After attending Christ For The Nations Institute in Dallas for two years, I returned home in 1994 to marry my waiting fiance. God has now blessed us with a daughter.

Since returning to my homeland, I have supervised the building and completion of 65 Native Churches. I believe God is so mightily blessing us because Mom Lindsay taught us students to pray daily for the peace (salvation) of Israel (Ps. 122:6), and to support God's chosen. *(Note: Each month Ram sends a financial gift to Israel from those churches.)*

—Ram Zango

Ram teaching in Ivory Coast

Determined to Reach Out

Duane and Jeane Vander Klok

A brand new, born-again Christian at age 20, a friend asked me to join him at a Bible college — Christ For The Nations Institute. I was hungry to gain more understanding of God. The excellent Bible teaching, the encouragement to establish a prayer life, and the atmosphere of praise and worship gave me a good, solid, spiritual foundation that has stayed with me to this day.

While at CFNI, I met my future wife, Jean. Together we wanted to reach out to the world. So upon graduation, we headed south. In Mexico, God continued our "Bible schooling." We learned to lean on His strength and faithfulness.

One day when Jean was baking a cake, the oven and pilot lights went out. We had no money to purchase more gas. God gave Jean a dose of bold faith, we laid hands on the empty cylinder, prayed and thanked God for His provision. Jean lit the pilots, and baked the cake. And, that blessed tank lasted longer than a normal full one!

God faithfully opened doors for us. We pastored a church in Guadalajara for a time. In 1978, we went to Hidalgo, where we strengthened believers, evangelized, and established churches. Then we returned to Guadalajara to teach in a Bible school.

After seven years in Mexico, God dropped a vision in my heart for a church in Michigan. I knew God wanted us there, so we moved. Soon I was invited to pastor a church of about 400 people.

Since January 1994, our church has grown to over 4,000, and many of our staff are CFNI graduates. Through a daily TV outreach to the U.S. and parts of Canada, we share practical wisdom for living from the Word. The Lord helped us establish 15 other churches in Michigan.

We have four children, ages 11 to 20, and continue to be "Bible schooled" —growing, learning and developing in many areas.

—***Duane Vander Klok***

The Vander Kloks' church in Grandville, Michigan

Learning the Ropes

Tim Sheets

When I was called to pastor in 1976, I quit my job and we sold our home. Then we packed up and headed for Christ For The Nations Institute in Dallas — my wife, Carol, baby daughter, Rachel, and I. It was one of the best decisions we ever made.

The foundations of ministry that I learned at CFNI are still in practice today. Each class offered what I needed, and the faculty was always prepared and anointed. Studying God's Word was exciting and fulfilling.

From Gordon Lindsay's books, I learned the importance of prayer. I still pray "violent prayers" and I have seen prayer move many mountains. I also learned the importance of writing. I have written three books: *Armed and Battle Ready, Being Led By The Spirit* and *Heaven Made Real*.

Through "Mom" Lindsay, the faculty and staff, I learned dedication and commitment to Christ. Their spirit of excellence inspired me as a student, and is still inspiring me today. I am proud to be a graduate of CFNI.

Following graduation, God called me to pastor 22 people. Living Word Church began with no buildings, no assets, and no money — it was time to use the principles I learned at CFNI. It wasn't always easy, but God came through; we started growing. Today, we own 46 acres, a beautiful 3,500-seat sanctuary, and an education building which is used for children's ministry, day care, a gymnasium, and a chapel. Thousands have been blessed through television, radio or one of our 43 outreaches. We started three other churches, now pastored by those we trained.

My family is 100% involved in the ministry —Carol is Administrator, Rachel and her godly husband, Mark, are both involved in our music ministry. Joshua, 15, is active in youth ministry and has a heart for God.

The seeds planted in my heart at CFNI have grown. Today, the fruit remains. God is faithful to His Word. To Him be all honor and praise. *(Note: Tim's brother, Dutch Sheets, a former CFNI instructor and an author, now pastors in Colorado Springs.)*

—Tim Sheets

Living Word Church in Middletown, Ohio

A God-Called Music Ministry

Arlene Friesen

In 1973, I was working as a public school music specialist, nearly halfway through a graduate degree program in my chosen field, music education. I had known the Lord since childhood and had always been involved in music ministry, including playing the piano and organ for some well-known ministries. Now, I found myself questioning my professional direction and sensing with strong conviction that I needed to devote some time to serious Bible study and prayer concerning God's call on my life. Some friends of mine were attending CFNI that year, and after a visit to the campus, I decided to enroll for one year.

Since the student body was small and musicians limited in number, I found myself very much involved again in music, but through teaching on praise and worship, and through the impartation of anointed ministries, I began to learn more about the purpose for musical gifts. As I found contentment in the presence of the Lord, that "one year" led to another and another. More opportunities for ministry, missions and teaching began to come my way. Later, I had the privilege of serving CFN in Germany for several years as the music director of the fledgling German school.

Little did I know that the decision to come to CFNI would impact my entire family, all of whom, parents and siblings, eventually attended CFNI as well. As chair of the Music Department at CFNI for the past nine years, I am amazed at the way the Lord's plan for my life has unfolded with blessings, challenges and fulfillment. Looking back I see His faithfulness in arranging my early training and background, then continuing to stretch and prune me to be of use for His Kingdom. "Commit your way to the LORD, trust also in Him, and He shall bring *it* to pass" (Psa. 37:5).

—*Arlene Friesen*

Gloria a Dios

Carla & Marco Barrientos

One month after I met Jesus, a godly veteran missionary, Wayne Myers, prayed for me to receive the Holy Spirit, and God's fire started burning within me. Wayne introduced me to CFNI and helped me go to Dallas. God used CFNI's wonderful family to profoundly impress my life in three main areas: 1) World vision: Through classes, guest speakers and fellowship with international students, my vision was radically enlarged; 2) Worship: The Lord took me to a new dimension in worship, and Jesus laid the foundation for my future; 3) Word: Being exposed daily to practical teaching of the Word was a great blessing. I developed a passion to obey God's Word.

Upon graduation in 1985, I served Jesus in Amistad Cristiana, my home fellowship in Mexico City. A burning desire to preach was not yet clear, so I served in the praise and worship ministry, taught home groups, and was involved in evangelism and counseling until the Lord opened more opportunities.

While at CFNI, and using borrowed equipment, the Lord allowed my brother, Luis, a few others and me to record two live praise and worship tapes in Spanish. We returned to Mexico City and began a small

recording company, "Leche y Miel Producciones" ("Milk and Honey Productions"). Tapes do not need a plane ticket, visa or passport. They reached Cuba, Argentina, Nicaragua, Colombia, Spain, and even Australia and Japan. Through these tapes, the Lord set people free from bondage, healing and renewing them. We have recorded 12 praise and worship projects — including one with Integrity Music, one with Vida (Life) Publishers, one with CanZion Producciones, and several more with our own label. We are currently partnering with CFN Music to produce Spanish versions of "Mighty River" and "Breath of Heaven." These tapes are expanding the powerful influence of CFN's wonderful ministry to the Spanish-speaking world.

I have had the opportunity to hold conferences, seminars and praise celebrations in stadiums with 40,000 present and I have ministered to handfuls of people in small mountain villages. In the 16 Spanish nations where I have ministered in music, people have been saved, healed and delivered. Many times I ask the Lord, "Why me? I am just a clay vessel." He answers, "But we have this treasure in earthen vessels, that the excellency of the power may be of God, and not of us!"

—*Marco Barrientos*

Sharing a Common Call

Eddie & Susan Hyatt

Eddie and Susan Hyatt met while students at Christ For The Nations Institute. They realized they shared a common call to follow the Lord. They were serious students who spent many hours in prayer and Bible study. Eddie also served as assistant pastor in the Assembly of God church in Chicota, Texas, and Sue worked in the CFNI cafeteria.

After their marriage in 1976, Eddie and Susan moved to New Brunswick, Canada, and pioneered a ministry that included a local congregation, a Bible school, a Christian school, and television and radio outreaches. In 1984, when God called them to further their education, they returned to Texas, enrolled in Southwestern Assemblies of God College, founded Hyatt International Ministries, and continued in full-time ministry.

Today they teach and preach, partner in research and writing, and conduct seminars. They are recognized Pentecostal/Charismatic historians and anointed Bible teachers. Eddie has served on the faculties of Oral Roberts University and Victory Bible institute in Tulsa, Oklahoma, as well as Zion Bible Institute in Barrington, Rhode Island. He currently serves on the faculties of Christian Life School of Theology in Columbus, Georgia, and the ORU School of Lifelong Education. Eddie is the author of *2000 years of Charismatic Christianity: A 21st Century Look at Church History from a Pentecostal/Charismatic Perspective*, and a manual entitled, *The Ministry of The Holy Spirit*.

Susan demonstrates a deep desire to see people develop their God-given potential. As a facilitator with particular interest in Bible schools, she has served as a consultant to leaders wanting to start Bible schools. As a ghost writer, she has helped several Christian leaders express their ideas effectively in written form. As an author and teacher, she is writing on Pentecostal/Charismatic issues and developing curriculum. Her first book, released in 1997, is *Where Are My Susannas?* Her first course consists of a textbook, audio-book, and teaching manual with study guide. It is entitled *In the Spirit We're Equal; The Spirit, the Bible, and Women, A Revival Perspective.*

The Hyatts participate in the Society for Pentecostal Studies, Christians for Biblical Equality, the Evangelical Theological Society, and Victory Fellowship of Ministries. Wherever they go, they are proud to be graduates of Christ For The Nations Institute.

A Faith-Walk

Dr. Harold & Patty Reents

In 1975, my wife, Patty, and I attended a Marriage Encounter weekend in the Catholic Church of which we were members. It changed our lives as we again submitted ourselves, individually and as a couple to the lordship of Jesus Christ. That weekend my wife and I became a team couple with Marriage Encounter. Later, we attended a training session for new Marriage Encounter team members, where my wife sovereignly received the baptism in the Holy Spirit. I later received the baptism in the Holy Spirit on a "Life in the Spirit" seminar in Springfield, Illinois.

The Lutheran couple who brought Marriage Encounter to our home town, attended a CFNI seminar. When they returned home, they resigned their jobs and left to enroll at CFNI. My wife and I and another couple drove caravan with them, helping to transport their things to Dallas. While on the campus, my wife heard the Holy Spirit say that we too would be attending CFNI. Two years later in 1978, she prayed, "Lord, if the desire to go to Bible school is not of You, please remove it from my heart; if it is of You, please set us free to go." Several weeks later, I was requested to resign from my position of superintendent of schools in which I had served 12 years. It was the most painful experience I have ever endured, yet I knew God's hand was in it.

My wife and I attended the summer seminar at CFNI in 1978, were water baptized in the Gospel Courts' pool, and applied to attend school. Later that summer, we put our home up for sale, left our two college-age sons standing on the porch, and with our three daughters, drove to Dallas to begin school. We were $100,000 in debt and I had no job. But we had perfect peace that He who called us would meet all our needs. We thought our house would sell immediately, but it didn't. During registration, Dr. Munroe, the Academic Dean, whom we had met during the seminar, requested I apply for the registrar's position that was coming open. For two months, the Lord sovereignly met all our needs as we awaited news about the position of registrar — a new walk of faith.

In October, I was given the position and allowed to attend chapel and classes and work in the afternoons. Then two years later, I was given the position of Academic Dean. I held that position until 1985, when we went to the mission field, where we started Bible schools in Thailand, Australia, and Malaysia. In 1992, we returned to the United States in obedience to the Lord, to await further guidance. He brought us back to CFNI January of 1994. At first I was alumni director and later became academic dean. My wife and I enjoy co-teaching Romans and Communion With God.

CFNI gave us a solid grounding in the Word of God. We learned to hear God's voice, the blessings of giving, and the importance of obedience. It's a place where our hearts are being healed and cleansed. We have had the privilege of traveling to many nations. The reputation of CFNI has opened many doors for us.

—*Dr. Harold Reents*

Jorge and Evangelina Lozano

Taking Worship to the Latin World

I met my wife Evangelina while we were both students at Christ For The Nations Institute. While there the Lord told me to learn everything I could because I was going to need it, so I took guitar and voice lessons with Arlene Friesen and Mary McLeod. Starting each morning with praise and worship taught us the importance of first ministering to the Lord, then to ourselves, and then to a lost world. Evangelina fondly remembers the teaching and morning worship services. She recalls Mrs. Lindsay's words, "If you didn't learn anything here, but you learned how to pray, your stay was worthwhile." Evangelina believes that everything we received at CFNI became the foundation for our ministry.

Upon graduation in 1978 we returned to Mexico City, where we were married six months later. We began home groups every day of the week and the Lord also began to use us in the area of praise and worship. After four years in Mexico City the Lord called us to the Baja

peninsula, to Caba San Lucas, where we started four churches. At that time I met Marcos Witt. Together with Marcos the Lord began to use us to travel all over Mexico doing praise and worship conferences. The country was affected and a change came through the teachings and new songs. In 1988, our pastors, Doctor Pardillo and his wife, invited us to go with them to Argentina to do some seminars. In Cordoba, where CFNI had a school, we taught for 15 days, and the Lord spoke to me through the Pardillos, and directly to my heart that He wanted me in that country. I opened the Bible and read Genesis 28:15, which confirmed His call. The Lord also spoke to my wife, and in three months our whole family was in Argentina.

Mrs. Lindsay named me the director of the school, and during the four years I served there, hundreds of students graduated. Then the Lord led me to leave the school. He began to open doors to our team in every country in Latin America, as well as the U.S. and Canada. My wife has been introducing tambourine and flags ministry, and I have traveled extensively holding worship seminars. Last year I went to Africa and this year doors in Europe began to open for us, and we have seen wonderful results. Over the years we have recorded nine praise and worship tapes.

Presently we are one of the pastors of "Cita con la Vida" (Date with Life), a wonderful church of about 5,000 people in Cordoba.

A worship conference with Jorge Lozano and Marcos Witt

Anna Jeanne Price and family (1997)

Providence and Privilege

Don and Anna Jeanne, June 28, 1952 in London

While I write this page on April 21, 1998 in my CFNI-campus apartment, a 50-year umbilical attachment to this ministry draws my thoughts back to mid-April 1948, and the groundswell of expedition crowding my young life. The first *Voice of Healing* magazine had been mailed, and recipients of those plain, yet power-packed pages were responding.

"Send 100 more!" ... "Please anoint the enclosed handkerchief." ... "Could my mother in Neosho be healed over the phone?" ... "Hello — I'd like a two-year subscription." ... (No ma'am, just send one dollar in case we don't last two years!) ... "Praise God! My cancer just fell off! I'll send it to you for a testimony."

Now we are beginning the second 50 years, and that alone is a testimony of the faith of my father, Jack Moore, and our friend, "Brother Gordon." They furnished the faith and drafted me to furnish the works in those PRE-electric typewriter days. Tomorrow I will submit this text to an efficient Editorial Department, where quiet computers, scanners, fax machines and photo copiers assist our congenial Headquarters staff in achieving the same goals set before my early workers: "Spread the good news — to as many people, in as many places, in as many ways as possible."

Today the "ways" have changed through modern technology; but not THE WAY. I consider it a privilege to still be connected with such an honorable cause, enjoying the fruits of earlier plantings while still able to sow into the fertile soil of today's youth.

"Privilege" may, in fact, be the defining term of my testimony. PRIVILEGED:

*To be born to a godly couple, depression-poor, but rich in faith (Mother Mildred prayed to have a girl — who would play the piano.)

*To be trained by the mother/teacher of famed pianist Van Cliburn, who was brought into our lives when Daddy built them a house near us

*To be providentially in place to work under Gordon Lindsay

*To be given, unexpectedly, a storybook wedding in the wing of Westminster Abbey

*To enjoy 14 years of marriage to Don Price, gifted musician-minister-missionary, devoted father of our beautiful five, before he was called home to heaven in the noontide of a notable life of service. (Having to leave the mission field of Thailand with my little ones and a very heavy heart was less than "privilege." But God's grace has brought us literally through many dangers, toils and snares.)

*To minister with lots of God's "generals" — and privates first-class, too

*To be associated with Freda Lindsay, peerless leader, beloved friend

*To know the satisfaction that devotion and servanthood brings to the heart — in this case to my father, whose sterling character and benevolence marked his many endeavors for God-sponsored success

And now in life's later seasons to still serve in two of those — CFN, and the church he planted, with my precious children and grands, is a priceless privilege.

Bishop Jack Wallace

A Great Big God

In 1983, I attended Christ For The Nations Institute out of a business background. I was young in the things of God, and seeking answers for my life. I knew a call of God was there, but how would it be formulated? In what direction would it take me?

My time at CFNI taught me that we have a big God — that He is big enough to embrace people of every color, kindred and tribe and that He is not so rigid and dogmatic that He cannot understand and embrace people of different opinions and backgrounds.

The diversity of guest speakers at CFNI was immense. But that taught me balance; it taught me to rightly divide the Word of God. It taught me to look at people's hearts more than their denominational background. It taught me how to trust God and to walk in faith in order to be a blessing, not just to be blessed. The principles I learned about servanthood, leadership and submission have been invaluable to me as a pastor.

The church I am pastoring today has been the fastest growing church in the Assemblies of God three out of the last four years. One of the reasons is the emphasis CFNI has placed on outreach. I learned to look for the needs in my community and then find a way to fill those needs.

CFNI had a profound impact on my life in the area of worship. I recognized that our church could reach that high standard with willing and open vessels.

The mark CFNI left on my life is indelible. It was a joy to be a student, and even more of a joy to return as a guest speaker myself. I feel confident that CFNI will continue to provide excellence in education — well-rounded and well-grounded, probably because it was well-founded! I am excited about the next 50 years. I believe CFNI has not even begun to see what God can do with this incredible vision He gave.

—Bishop Jack Wallace

To Dallas and Beyond

Robert, Patti and Jason Conn

Robert and I met in Bible college, and in 1967 we married. In 1983, after having spent a decade in ministry, giving unreservedly of our time and talents, we were exhausted. We were at a crossroad in our lives, and we were seeking God's direction.

One day I came across a book written by my great Aunt Freda — "My Diary Secrets." Within 24 hours, the direction we had been seeking was ours. The Lord spoke clearly to each of us as we read the book: Go to Christ For The Nations. When our 10-year-old son, Jason, was ready to leave his friends and his dog behind, we knew God had touched his heart as well. So we sold most of our belongings and left the state of Washington for Dallas, Texas.

I began work at CFN in the missions department about the same time Robert started classes at the institute. Robert thoroughly enjoyed the practical training he received, but his favorite part of the day was chapel. He loved starting each morning with praise and worship. His soul was refreshed and his vision renewed during his two years at CFNI.

Over the next nine years we lived on campus, Jason was ministered to through CFN's fabulous children's and youth ministries. Plus he made friends from many nations and thoroughly enjoyed the availability of the swimming pools and the gym. He has grown up to be a fine young man with a heart for the Lord and for people. He is currently in medical school, and this fall will begin his clinical rotations.

Eventually, I was transferred from the missions department to editorial and Robert joined the CFN staff. Being on the staff at CFN has given Robert and me the opportunity to serve the Lord with our individual God-given abilities. For the last eight years, I have been the managing editor. I love writing, researching, teaching and organizing, so I find much satisfaction in fulfilling my varied responsibilities. I have had the privilege of working closely with both Freda and Dennis Lindsay. One of my greatest joys has been assisting Dennis in producing his Creation Science series.

Robert, too, has found great fulfillment at CFN. He loves teaching, encouraging others, lots of variety, and pioneering and administrating projects. He started out as the assistant dean of families. While in that position he pioneered the ACE School of Tomorrow, which is a double blessing. It not only provides an on-campus school for the children of students and staff, but training for CFNI students, who can then work in or start an ACE school in some part of the world. Over the years, Robert has held several positions in addition to being an instructor. In 1995, he launched an exciting program: a proactive admissions program. Presently, he is director of admissions and of CFN's deparament of public safety.

In our respective departments, Robert and I have the delightful opportunity to labor with dedicated co-workers, many of them students, each with a unique personality and special calling. We are humbled that we have had the opportunity to be a part of CFN — a ministry that reaches far beyond Dallas, Texas, to 120 nations of the world.

—*Patti Conn*

The Vision

WHAT AN EXCITING TIME TO celebrate 50 years of successful ministry, with the year 2000 just ahead. Christ For The Nations' leadership is strategizing for the new millennium — making plans to train world changers to take the message of Christ to the unreached people on every continent of planet Earth. We anticipate that the dynamic foundation of integrity and vision that has been laid in the last 50 years will result in a spiritually synergistic force that will impact every nation for Christ in the 21st century.

Dennis Gordon Lindsay
Chairman of the Board,
President and CEO

Vision for a New Generation

The Lord first began to impart vision into my spirit when I rejoined the Christ For The Nations ministry after serving on the mission field for several years. Vision flooded my young heart and mind, and I would passionately write out the thoughts and sketch the concepts, then submit them to the leadership in eager anticipation. When my visions didn't receive the expected acceptance, I was reminded of the word of the Lord to Habbakuk: "For the vision is yet for an appointed time" (2:3). So I waited.

Patience was developed in me during those early years. A refining and maturing process was working in me to test my endurance and my faith. I discovered that there is a peace that comes over the soul as a result of learning to wait in faith. Vision combined with patience and faith instills confidence that just as surely as God promised seedtime and harvest, the seed that He has planted in the good soil of your heart will grow and bring forth fruit. "Though it tarries, wait for it; because it will surely come" (Hab. 2:3).

When the time came to build the Student Center, the Lord had already given the plans to me. Only a few changes were needed, and then we were able to proceed quickly with the project because God had placed the concept in my heart many years earlier.

The Lord often builds on the experiences of the past to equip us for the future. As a young couple, Ginger and I were powerfully impacted by Youth With A Mission. By their invitation, we went on an extended biblical studies tour of Israel. We were discipled in Switzerland, and then we ministered for some time in Spain. During much of this time we were drawn to the mountains. Many of them were stark and foreboding. But others were majestic and serene. We loved the exhilaration of reaching the summits, and we were thrilled with the clarity of vision that the mountain tops provided.

The Word of God records powerful experiences on mountains in the lives of many of God's servants... Abraham, Moses, Caleb, Elijah and others. And throughout the Jesus' ministry, mountains were prominent: He preached His greatest sermon on a mountain. He often prayed on a mountain. He was transfigured on a

An artistic rendition of the new World Missions Training Center
(Phase I — the basement — is finished.)

Vision for a New Generation

mountain, died on a mountain, and He will appear again on a mountain.

At CFN, we are facing a whole mountain range of challenges ahead. But the Lord has given us a great climbing party… our competent and dedicated ministry team and generous, prayerful supporters like you. Though the ascent to the top of each mountain will be a struggle, we know the fellowship along the way will be sweet and the victory measured in eternal values.

WORLD MISSIONS TRAINING CENTER

Our first challenge will be to complete the next phase of construction on the World Missions Training Center. That project has been on hold because just as we finished the first phase… the basement, we had an unparalleled opportunity to acquire 152 apartments needed for our students, alumni and staff.

But now it is time to move forward on the center. It will provide the facilities we need to properly train our national and international students for the mission fields of the world.

The center will also provide a Historical Gallery to display for students and visitors the story of Christ For The Nations… the heritage of God's blessings on the ministry. It will house our progressive Youth Department, including our School of Youth Ministries and Youth For The Nations. It will be a cultural research center, a creation science laboratory, a house of prayer, and a learning environment where the voice of God can be heard through anointed teaching. As growing numbers of believers are responding to the call of God in these last days, we must be prepared to train and commission them into the harvest.

STUDENT ENROLLMENT INCREASES

God has used CFNI to mold the character and spiritually equip some of today's prominent spiritual leaders. Yet many believers worldwide have not heard about CFNI. We must let them know of the great training institute the Lord has established here in Dallas. To facilitate the big vision the Lord has given us, He has provided the housing and some of the finest, most dedicated staff found anywhere. With the Great Commission being more urgent than ever, we are preparing for the largest, multicultural enrollment in our history. We are ready to train world changers for the new millennium.

BROADCAST MEDIA MINISTRIES

Recent years have evidenced a radio revival. When television and videos began to dominate our entertainment-crazed culture, many assumed that radio would become a communications relic. Surprisingly, it enjoys an even greater popularity today. With our anointed music distinctive, we are anticipating providing a regular broadcast resource — programs about praise and worship to bless the body of Christ over the radio waves.

Television is such an important media in our society that it cannot be neglected. Quality programming which shares the dynamic impact that a trained and dedicated army of CFNI alumni is having on the world is a vision whose time has come. "WorldChangers" is our new half-hour program. Unique in the Christian media, it

CFNI's 75-acre campus in Dallas (situated between two major thoroughfares) — our Jerusalem — must be properly maintained so we can continue to reach the world.

Vision for a New Generation

is designed both to minister and to publicize the tremendous opportunities available at CFNI for spiritual growth and ministry training.

In our Golden Jubilee, we are launching both television and radio ministries. We believe the Lord will use these means to fulfill his purposes for Christ For The Nations in the 21st century.

CAMPUS DEVELOPMENT

As we embark on the new millennium, we must be commendable stewards of the world ministry headquarters the Lord has established here in Dallas. This is our Jerusalem. If we neglect the home base, our ministry to the uttermost parts of the earth will begin to diminish.

For several years we have been concentrating on needs around the world and have given very little attention to maintaining the facilities here at home base. A planned approach to renovation will be implemented over the next several years.

MINISTRIES TO THE WORLD

"Christ For The Nations... It's more than our name; it's our mission!" That slogan reflects the ministry's goal: to fulfill the Great Commission. Our heritage includes helping worthy ministries around the world in their endeavors. We not only plan to continue that through the Native Church Foundation and the Native Literature program, we expect to intensify our efforts as the Lord provides the resources.

Trained nationals are more readily accepted by their own people than outsiders, thus are more effective in reaching them for Christ. We

have already begun to focus on expanding and strengthening our international Association of Bible Schools. We already have 40 associated schools, and our goal is to have 50 by the year 2000.

The international student scholarship program must be funded. We would like to double our international student population here at the Dallas institute over the next few years.

As individuals and churches catch the vision to invest in the lives of those who have the potential to become spiritual leaders in the nations of the world, we will be able to provide the training and commissioning that will equip them to become world changers.

Caleb of old knew the secret to success. He said, "If the Lord shall be with me, then shall I be able." The Lord has been stirring our hearts with new vision. It is time to press boldly forward in obedience to His prompting.

We invite you to join us as we climb each challenging mountain of campus and ministry expansion. With your help, we can make it!

We are excited about what God has in store for Christ For The Nations in the years to come. He has injected mountain-climbing faith into our spirits.

If you, too, are sensing that faith rising within, I am confident that you will say with me, "GIVE ME THIS MOUNTAIN!"

— *** Dennis G. Lindsay ***
Chairman of the Board,
President and CEO

President Lindsay's vision of a Plaza of the Nations —
where students and staff can walk or sit as they pray for the nations of the world

Prophecy...

Not many days from here, says the Lord, there is coming a fresh wind. And there will be an overturning and an undertaking. ... Up out of the people will come a move of God ... what you didn't expect.

For you have only seen first drops, but for you who have known what the true rain is all about, God says ... what was in the former is going to be multiplied in the latter, and you're going to see it.

God says there are going to be miracles. ... You're going to see what you have dreamed of, what you have known about. But now it's going to happen; you're going to see it with your eyes. Not only will you send Christ to the nations, but they will come [to you] from all over the world. ...

God says this is a new day! ... There's a breath of life being breathed, and suddenly you will be overtaken!

Prophecy given regarding CFN
Women's Ministers' Invitational Conference, January 1998
Shirley Arnold

Our Vision is Even Stronger Than our Heritage!